Beyond Hiroshima

For Lynn Thurston
with best wishes

Douglas Roche
Aug 24/06

Beyond Hiroshima

Douglas Roche

NOVALIS

Cover design: Audrey Wells
Cover image: Photo.com
Layout: Christiane Lemire, Audrey Wells

Business Office:
Novalis
49 Front Street East, 2nd Floor
Toronto, Ontario, Canada
M5E 1B3

Phone: 1-800-387-7164
Fax: 1-800-204-4140
E-mail: cservice@novalis-inc.com
www.novalis.ca

Library and Archives Canada Cataloguing in Publication

Roche, Douglas, 1929–
    Beyond Hiroshima / Douglas Roche.
Includes index.

ISBN 2-89507-670-7

    1. Nuclear disarmament.

JZ5675.R6 2005   327.1'747   C2005-904692-9

Printed in Canada.

We acknowledge the financial support of the Government of Canada through the Book Publishing Industry Development Program (BPIDP) for our publishing activities.

5 4 3 2 1   09 08 07 06 05

For the hibakusha of Hiroshima and Nagasaki,

who have suffered and taught the world

Peace, peace to the far and near, says the Lord,

And I will heal them.

Isaiah 57:19

Contents

Part IV: Reviving Hope for a Nuclear Weapons–Free World

Acknowledgements

I have learned about nuclear weapons from many sources. My visits to Hiroshima and Nagasaki and interviews with the *hibakusha* seared the horror of nuclear weapons into my mind. My experience as Canada's Ambassador for Disarmament and, in 1988, Chairman of the United Nations Disarmament Committee gave me a deep insight into the diplomatic process. In 1985, I led the Canadian Delegation to the Third Review Conference of the Non-Proliferation Treaty (NPT) and, since then, have followed NPT work closely and written extensively on it.

I have many mentors to whom I am grateful, particularly the late Bill Epstein; Sir Joseph Rotblat, a scientist with the Manhattan Project who renounced nuclear weapons and founded Pugwash, later sharing with it the Nobel Peace Prize; and Jayantha Dhanapala, president of the 1995 NPT Review and Extension Conference, who later became Under-Secretary-General for Disarmament Affairs at the United Nations. I am honoured that Jayantha Dhanapala has written the foreword to this book.

Numerous colleagues in nuclear disarmament work from non-governmental organizations have helped me over the years. I have learned from many, but I would be remiss not to thank Ernie Regehr, former executive director of Project Ploughshares, and Jonathan Granoff, President of the Global Security Institute, for their unflagging support. Leaders in the Canadian movement to abolish nuclear weapons have inspired me, particularly Dr. Mary Wynne Ashford, Bev Delong, Debbie Grisdale, Judith Berlyn, Murray Thomson,

Robin Collins, Steve Staples, Sarah Estabrooks, Dr. Joanna Santa Barbara and Macha MacKay.

The Middle Powers Initiative (MPI) team, particularly my fellow executive members, David Krieger, Karel Koster, Alice Slater and Michael Christ, along with Program Manager Zack Allen, combine deep knowledge and highly effective political activism. I owe a special debt of gratitude to Alyn Ware. Rob Green, Kate Dewes and Jennifer Simons helped me and the MPI enormously in its early days. Pugwash Conferences on Science and World Affairs, led by Prof. M.S. Swaminathan, Paolo Cotta-Ramusino and Jeffrey Boutwell, provides excellent material on the nuclear weapons situation. I also work closely with the Canadian Pugwash Group Executive: Adele Buckley, Walter Dorn, Erika Simpson, Sergei Plekhanov, Derek Paul, Peter Walker and Peter Meincke.

In preparing this book, Aaron Braaten, my research assistant, provided invaluable help finding statistics and documents and critiquing the manuscript. He also prepared the list of websites at the back of the book. All website addresses were accurate as of July 12, 2005.

The graphs were prepared by Khalid Yaqub, who designed my website (www.douglasroche.ca), and who is now preparing a PowerPoint presentation of the book, as he did for my 2003 book, *The Human Right to Peace* (Novalis).

John Burroughs, Executive Director, Lawyers' Committee on Nuclear Policy, read the manuscript in draft form and saved me from several mistakes. Any remaining errors are my responsibility.

Bonnie Payne, my assistant for fifteen years, processed the manuscript through several drafts with her unfailing competence and good cheer.

Again, Kevin Burns, Commissioning Editor at Novalis, gave me the understanding, criticism and confidence that I value so much in an editor. Anne Louise Mahoney,

Managing Editor, was very helpful. Amy Heron copy edited the text with care.

In Hiroshima, Mayumi Yamane, Supervisor, Hiroshima City Training Institute, gave me excellent guidance.

The support of my wife, Patricia McGoey, occupies a special place in my heart. I am also grateful for the support of my children, Evita, Douglas Francis, Mary Anne and Patricia.

Deep concern for the future life of my grandchildren, Isabelle and Nicholas, gave me the deepest motivation to write this book. When I turned 75 in 2004, my long-standing parliamentary colleague David MacDonald said at a celebratory dinner that, far from being over, my most important work was still ahead. I hope this book has proven him right.

Douglas Roche
Edmonton
August 11, 2005

Foreword

by Jayantha Dhanapala

In May 2005, the states parties to the Treaty on the Non-Proliferation of Nuclear Weapons (NPT) – the most widely subscribed-to treaty in the world, next to the U.N. Charter – gathered at the United Nations in New York for the NPT Review Conference. They met for four weeks amidst grave and widespread doubts over the continued relevance and viability of the Treaty as a bulwark against proliferation – and the only legal commitment on the part of five nuclear weapon states to disarm and finally eliminate their deadly arsenals. Those doubts appeared justified when the states parties left New York without a final document agreeing on conclusions about the NPT's past performance or its future.

The world cannot afford the luxury of a passive acceptance of the outcome of this NPT Review Conference. Several governments, supported by civil society, continue to work for nuclear disarmament and nuclear non-proliferation. Among the most dedicated and valiant fighters for these twin causes is Douglas Roche, whom I first met at the 1985 NPT Review Conference in Geneva. Since then, I have been deeply impressed by the sustained sincerity and passionate zeal he has brought to the debate in the Canadian Senate; in the United Nations; in the Middle Powers Initiative, which he launched; in numerous other international and national forums; and on the lecture circuit, where his advocacy of nuclear disarmament has been consistent and cogent.

In a year of anniversaries, Douglas Roche commemorates the most dismal of them – the sixtieth anniversary of the Hiroshima and Nagasaki bombings. The hiatus between state policies and civil society positions, which was demonstrated by the march of 40,000 civil society activists in New York on May 1, 2005, demands new initiatives. *Beyond Hiroshima* explains the background and rationale for this position. The author walks us through all the arguments and through the history of previous efforts to achieve nuclear disarmament, updating us on today's dangers of nuclear terrorism and the use of space for future wars. Roche builds up a political, moral and religious case, drawing on his thirty years' experience working on nuclear issues as a parliamentarian, diplomat and educator. Readers will profit from his unique insights.

"If it ain't broke, don't fix it" says homespun American folk wisdom. Well, the NPT may not be entirely "broke," but it clearly has many holes. Some of the holes were deliberately built in at its creation. Other holes are congenital – like holes in the heart. The Procrustean task of merging President Eisenhower's lofty vision of "Atoms for Peace" with the prohibition on the development of nuclear weapons led to Articles III and IV of the NPT. The focus of recent revelations and comment on the NPT has been on this aspect of the Treaty.

Then there are the holes that are revealed through experience and the wear and tear of several years. The clandestine program of Iraq, which was revealed and eliminated by the UN Security Council's inspectors, led to the International Atomic Energy Agency (IAEA)'s "93 plus two" negotiating process. This process resulted in the 1997 Additional Protocol, which aimed to close the loopholes in the IAEA's safeguards agreements that were exposed by the Saddam regime. Another issue to address is what to do about states parties whose actions go against the treaty, then want to leave the NPT. Can the Security Council prohibit states from leaving the NPT? If so, will this apply to all treaties, or only to weapons of mass destruction treaties, and then only for small, troublesome states? A related problem is what to do about states parties that are found to have violated the NPT and want to come back into the NPT. In a climate already highly charged after the tragedy of 9/11, the revelations of a sophisticated network of underworld commerce in nuclear weapon technology and materials by private individuals such as Pakistan's Dr. A.Q. Khan, along with the danger that this activity may include terrorist groups, add urgency to these questions. The Security Council has acted unanimously to adopt a resolution that aims at preventing weapons of mass destruction from falling into the hands of terrorist groups.

A spate of proposals to remedy the current situation of the NPT is available for the states parties to the NPT to consider. They range from the February 11, 2005, speech of President George W. Bush, to proposals advanced by the Director-General of the IAEA, commentators such as former senior U.S. Administration officials, and others. Some proposals have already been implemented unilaterally in the form of aggressive counter-proliferation measures, such as the Proliferation Security Initiative (PSI), by a group of countries. Of these, Director-General ElBaradei seeks to understand the reasons why non–nuclear weapon states would want nuclear weapons. He also uniquely urges the international community to "abandon the unworkable notion that it is morally reprehensible for some countries to pursue weapons of mass destruction yet morally acceptable for others to rely on them for security and indeed to continue to refine their capacities and postulate plans for their use."

Simply put, there are no good nukes or bad nukes. Nor are there right hands and wrong hands for nuclear weapons. In a globalized world where there are no leak-proof boundaries or walls against transnational physical or intellectual property transfers, we can no longer sustain an apartheid world of nuclear weapon states and non–nuclear weapon states – least of all by the use of force, however extreme.

Only a consensus that is forged *now* can save the NPT, which was extended indefinitely in 1995, in a carefully crafted consensus under my presidency, to ensure a safer and more predictable world. That hope was enhanced by the consensus reached at the 2000 NPT Review Conference – after the 1996 Advisory Opinion of the International Court of Justice and the 1998 nuclear device explosions of India and Pakistan – which established thirteen steps towards fulfilling the aims of the NPT. The outcome of the 2005 NPT Review Conference must therefore be seen as a temporary setback, with Douglas Roche's book providing a clear vision of a nuclear weapon–free world and how we can get there.

Jayantha Dhanapala is a former United Nations Under-Secretary-General for Disarmament Affairs. During his term as Ambassador of Sri Lanka to the United States, he presided over the historic NPT Review and Extension Conference of 1995.

Introduction

That Day Will Come

When the first atomic bombs destroyed Hiroshima and Nagasaki in 1945, it could hardly have been imagined that 60 years later more than 30,000 nuclear weapons would be in existence. The Cold War is long over, but half the world's population still lives under a government that brandishes nuclear weapons. More than $12 trillion has so far been spent on these instruments of mass murder, which is a theft from the poorest people in the world. The present nuclear weapons crisis has, in fact, led to the opening of the Second Nuclear Age.

First, we must understand the dimensions of the crisis. The long-standing nuclear weapons states — the United States, Russia, the United Kingdom, France and China — are making nuclear weapons permanent instruments of their military doctrines. India, Pakistan and Israel have joined the nuclear club. North Korea is trying to get into it. Iran is suspected of trying to acquire the capacity to convert nuclear fuel into nuclear weapons. NATO is maintaining U.S. nuclear weapons on the soil of six European countries, and the U.S. is preparing "reliable replacement" warheads with new military capabilities.

The U.S. and Russia have put new emphasis on the war-fighting role of nuclear weapons. The nuclear weapons states refuse to give up their arsenals, and feign surprise that other nations, seeing that nuclear weapons have become the currency of power in the modern world, are trying to acquire them. So are terrorists. No major city in the world is safe from the threat of a nuclear attack. The risk of accident multiplies daily. All these are characteristics of the Second Nuclear Age.

Thinking that the nuclear weapons problem went away with the end of the Cold War, much of the public is oblivious to the new nuclear dangers. U.N. Secretary-General Kofi Annan is trying to warn governments and the public, but few are listening. In the case of many politicians, they do not even know that they *don't* know about the greatest threat to human security the world has ever faced. They do not recognize the continued existence of enormous stocks of nuclear weapons, most with a destructive power many times greater than that of the atomic bombs that destroyed Hiroshima and Nagasaki.

Nuclear weapons are instruments of pure evil. A nuclear explosion, either by design or accident, would kill a massive number of people, create international chaos and cripple the world economy.

Nuclear weapons are devoid of the slightest shred of moral legitimacy. Prominent jurists consider their use illegal in any possible circumstance. The nuclear weapons states are deliberately undermining the rule of law by maintaining them.

It staggers the imagination to consider what the enormous sums spent on nuclear forces could have done for education, health and other requisites for the development of peoples everywhere. The United States spends $110 million *every day* maintaining its nuclear forces and is seeking money from Congress for new ones. This is driving world military spending, which exceeded $1 trillion in 2004, a 20 per cent increase in two years.

Governments have thrown democracy out the window in their zeal for armaments. Nowhere have citizens clamoured for nuclear weapons. Rather, governments have either imposed them or manipulated public opinion to get people to quietly accept them. A 2002 poll of citizens in 11 countries, including the U.S. and Canada, showed that 86 per cent of people either strongly agree (72 per cent) or agree to some extent (14 per cent) that all nations should sign a treaty to ban all nuclear weapons. Governments are ignoring this opinion; the public, except for core groups of activists, is not actively demanding that governments move towards such a treaty. Instead, the public is saying, we should cure the worst of poverty and restore the environment.

In this new nuclear age, when public attention is sapped by the repercussions of the terrorist attacks of September 11, 2001, including terrorist attacks on the mass transit systems of Madrid and London, the entire framework for nuclear disarmament is in danger of being swept away. The month-long 2005 Review Conference of the Non-Proliferation Treaty ended in deadlock between the nuclear haves and have-nots. The Comprehensive Nuclear Test Ban Treaty is stagnating. Strategic arms reduction by the U.S. and Russia, which together possess 96 per cent of all nuclear weapons, is atrophying. The work of the Conference on Disarmament in Geneva is paralyzed. Time is running out. The Pugwash Conferences on Science and World Affairs, which won the 1995 Nobel Peace Prize for its work on nuclear disarmament, has noted the following:

> The difficulties and even the possibility of a collapse of the nuclear non-proliferation regime, the weakening of the taboos in place since 1945 on the use of nuclear weapons, coupled with the dangers of a terrorist group detonating a nuclear explosive device, combine to produce a recipe for unmitigated disaster.

Global Public Opinion on Prohibition of Nuclear Weapons

*Do you agree or disagree, strongly or somewhat, that
all countries should sign a treaty that prohibits all nuclear weapons?*

	Agree		Disagree		Don't know**
	Strongly	Somewhat	Somewhat	Strongly	
Nuclear powers					
USA	61%	15%	10%	14%	0%
Russia*	78%	13%	4%	1%	4%
France	72%	18%	5%	4%	0%
UK	72%	12%	7%	7%	2%
India*	66%	12%	3%	4%	14%
Non-nuclear powers					
Germany	88%	5%	3%	3%	0%
Brazil*	89%	7%	2%	2%	1%
Canada	83%	8%	4%	5%	0%
South Korea	69%	18%	9%	3%	2%
Japan	77%	20%	2%	1%	0%
South Africa*	53%	22%	5%	5%	14%
*urban samples					**Percentages are rounded

Data from a public opinion poll conducted from February to March 2002 by the Liu Institute for the Study of Global Issues at the University of British Columbia in co-operation with The Asahi Shimbun, Japan. The international research firm Ipsos-Reid fielded the survey, which canvassed the opinion of 6,036 adult respondents. Reprinted with permission.

It is in times of crisis that the nuclear disarmament movement has been strongest. This was true in the 1980s when there were massive protests against NATO's deployment of nuclear weapons in Europe. Today, the Abolition 2000 movement is gaining strength, and the number of expert non-governmental activists in dialogue with governments is growing. Solid work is being done to lay the political, legal and technical foundation for a nuclear weapons–free world. This work appears to be overshadowed by the magnitude of the nuclear crisis, but the quality of the work gives hope that the world, once awakened, will move beyond a repetition of the horrors of Hiroshima and Nagasaki.

The framework for a nuclear weapons–free world is coming into view, even as the daily news seems discouraging. It is perhaps paradoxical that those with vision can see a light even in the darkness of the moment.

My experience tells me that it is reasonable to hope for and work for a world beyond Hiroshima. As a parliamentarian, diplomat and educator, I have worked on nuclear disarmament issues for more than 30 years. I understand the lassitude and obstinacy of governments all too well. But I also see the positive developments taking place in civil society: an increasing number of highly informed and deeply committed activists are co-operating with like-minded governments to improve human security. The Anti-Personnel Landmines Treaty, the International Criminal Court and the new surge of government commitment to international aid have come about because of civil society's input into government machinery.

We stand on the threshold of the construction of a viable plan for a nuclear weapons–free world resulting from the active co-operation of knowledgeable leaders of civil society working with those politicians and officials of like-minded governments who truly want to move forward.

The day will arrive when either nuclear weapons are abolished or the world is devastated by a nuclear attack. One or the other will happen. No person, informed on the gravity of the situation, can deny it.

PART I

The Plea and the Paralysis

1

Hiroshima:
A Statement on the Future

At 8:15 a.m. on August 6, 2005, 55,000 people stood in the Hiroshima Peace Memorial Park for a moment of silence to remember the atomic devastation that had occurred precisely 60 years before. A bell tolled. The mood was sombre. A minute later, hundreds of doves were released. They swooped over the crowd. Our eyes lifted to the blue sky.

The scene was flashed around the world, and suddenly Hiroshima was back, perhaps for only a moment, in world consciousness. Tadatoshi Akiba, Mayor of Hiroshima, went to the microphone to speak of the "shared lamentation" of the day that must turn into a campaign to rid the world of nuclear weapons forever. The speeches went on and the heat of the day became oppressive. I looked around. Ahead of me was a group of survivors of the bombing and their relatives. Behind me were young musicians from Boston who would play at a concert that evening. Two children came to the stage, crying out for a peaceful world.

Suddenly, I had a flashback to August 6, 1945. I was back at the kitchen table in our family home in Ottawa, a boy of sixteen. The radio announcer led off the morning news with a story about a new kind of bomb that had just been dropped on Japan. The destruction was so massive, the announcer said, that Canadian officials were predicting the war in the Pacific would be over in a matter of days. My parents smiled; I would be spared having to go to war. Then we went uptown to join the street celebrations. The war was over! I had never seen such joy.

My teenage life continued. Studies, sports, girlfriends – all the preoccupations of youth seemed to preclude serious thinking about the issues of war and peace. Next were marriage, young children and the beginnings of middle age. It was only then that Hiroshima, and Nagasaki, where the second atomic bomb was dropped three days after the first, entered my consciousness. My thoughts were jumbled.

Japan had first bombed Pearl Harbor in 1941, bringing on the war in the Pacific. Though World War II in Europe had come to a close in May 1945, the Japanese would not surrender. Maybe the Americans were right to use the powerful new atomic bomb to end the war quickly and save lives that would otherwise have been lost in an invasion. But what about the immense suffering inflicted on the people of Hiroshima and Nagasaki? Surely that was wrong. And what about the continued development of thousands of new nuclear weapons? Aren't they compounding new dangers? This is how my mind fluctuated until, some 25 years ago, I first went to Hiroshima and Nagasaki to see for myself what atomic bombs really meant.

The sights horrified me. Though both cities were in the process of being rebuilt, the museums contained graphic descriptions of human suffering I had never thought possible. I talked to the *hibakusha*, the survivors, and their stories put a human face on what had been just statistics. What does it mean when 140,000 people die in a blast and from the resulting radiation? I could begin to envision it when talking to Akihiro Takahashi, who, as a fourteen-year-old boy, crawled over rubble to soak his searing skin in the Motoyasu

River. Akihiro later became the Director of the Hiroshima Peace Memorial Museum. We corresponded. I returned to Hiroshima a few times, each time experiencing at deeper levels a combination of humbleness and hope. I felt deep shame and anger at so much human suffering caused by war; and I felt hope when I saw how the people of Hiroshima had rebuilt their lives on the principle of going forward, not dwelling on the past.

Now I was back in Hiroshima, a city of 1.1 million people and many skyscrapers, for the 60th anniversary. The morning ceremony came to an end with a children's choral performance. An hour later, I went to a meeting with my friend Akihiro Takahashi, who once more told his story. As with many of us who have jumped into the electronic age, Akihiro was now using a PowerPoint presentation of paintings depicting his life in the hours following the bombing. The hideous sights of burnt skin were riveting. The woman beside me, an activist with an American non-governmental organization, started crying. Afterwards, Akihiro called me and a few others to the stage. He draped a white and red lei made of paper cranes over my shoulders. "Remember," he whispered to me. Paper cranes were made famous in Japan by Sadako Sasaki, a little girl who developed acute leukemia from the Hiroshima blast. She had faith in the popular belief that folding a thousand paper cranes would make your wishes come true. Even when she was in terrible pain, she folded more and more of them, hoping to get well. But within eight months she died. Her classmates took over the paper crane project, and a monument to Sadako was built near the A-Bomb Dome, the epicentre of the blast.

The A-Bomb Dome is the most recognizable symbol of Hiroshima. It topped the Hiroshima Prefectural Industrial Promotion Hall, a splendid building in its day and a focal point for artists and actors. The shell of the building was virtually the only edifice left standing after the attack. Now, as a World Heritage site, it is propped up and brilliantly lit at night. Beside it flows the Motoyasu River, where I headed in the evening, with huge crowds, to float a paper lantern with a peace message inscribed on it. Thousands of lanterns floating down the river made a statement more powerful than most speeches.

The Spirit of Hiroshima

The magnitude of the tragedy inflicted by the atomic bomb convinced the people of Hiroshima that "the human race and nuclear weapons cannot coexist indefinitely." Thus, the city of Hiroshima became a global symbol, a city striving to eliminate nuclear weapons and bring about genuine and lasting world peace.

Memories of August 6 and the days of suffering that followed are extremely painful for the survivors, but many regularly overcome their heart-rending grief to tell others of their A-bomb experience because they want to convey to the world their conviction that nuclear weapons must never, under any circumstances, be used again.

It is the mission of the A-bombed city to spread the "spirit of Hiroshima" throughout the world, arousing international public opinion and doing everything in its power to bring into being a world that is truly at peace.

The Spirit of Hiroshima

Published by Hiroshima Peace Memorial Museum

I think that is what Hiroshima has become: a statement. It is not simply a commemoration of the dead, though that is a central element of its heritage. The city also projects a vision of peace, starting with raw courage. To contrast the vibrant life of the modern city – with its wide avenues, crowded shopping areas and cultural exhibits – with the bestial conditions of a life, if it can be called that, so grotesque that wartime censors would not allow images from the city to be sent out to the world, is to marvel at the human spirit. If any oppressed people have ever "overcome," it is surely the people of Hiroshima and their counterparts in Nagasaki.

The statement the museum makes is unambiguous. The exhibit opens with split-screen images of nuclear testing and warnings that the only way to guarantee the survival of the human species is to eliminate nuclear weapons. We see a

model of Hiroshima as it was after the devastation. Within
a two-kilometre radius, everyone died. They were perhaps
the lucky ones, for the survivors endured a hell on earth,
with many dying over the next few months.

Why did all this happen? The exhibits show in detail the
development of U.S. policy to use the new atomic bomb
on Japan once it was ready. All that is past, the exhibits proclaim. What counts now is present and future U.S. policy.
The U.S. and the other nuclear weapons states are warned
to stop making nuclear weapons a centrepiece of modern
military doctrine. One exhibit makes the point that the total
destructive nuclear force of the nuclear weapons states was
22,000 megatons at its peak during the Cold War, or 1.38
million times the power of the Hiroshima bomb. Thus, the
museum has converted a commemoration of the past into
a blunt warning to humanity to face up to what is required
to prevent future Hiroshimas. A plaque proclaims:

> Since entering the 21st century, rather than evinc-
> ing respect for nuclear disarmament based on
> international discussion, the U.S. Administration
> is constructing a missile defence system and other
> U.S.-centered security measures. Since the terrorist
> attacks of September 11, 2001, the U.S. has identi-
> fied both nation states and terrorist organizations
> as threats and is shifting to a strategy that overtly
> includes the use of nuclear weapons under certain
> circumstances. Such trends continue to batter the
> treaty structure governing international arms control
> and disarmament.

I went to many events observing the 60th anniversary:
conferences for nuclear weapons specialists, a gathering of
8,000 representatives of non-governmental organizations, a
rally of 3,000 youth and a special Mass at the World Peace
Memorial Cathedral attended by a score of Asian bishops.

Throughout, the tone, while sombre, was not one of bitterness but of warning: humanity must lift itself up from the spectre of extinction by nuclear weapons. Out of the suffering, Hiroshima says, we must see the dangers and, once we have absorbed this, be energized with hope to build a world of peace. This was the note struck by Pope John Paul II when he visited Hiroshima on February 25, 1981. His handwritten message read: "God's hope is one of peace, not one of pain." At the entranceway to the museum, a huge marble statue of hands reaching out for each other contains this inscription from Pope John Paul II:

> War is the work of man.
> War is the destruction of human life.
> War is death.
> To remember the past is to
> 	commit oneself to the future.
> To remember Hiroshima is to
> 	abhor nuclear war.
> To remember Hiroshima is to
> 	commit oneself to peace.

This theme was continued by the Japanese Catholic bishops who, in a statement issued for the 60th anniversary, said they must be true to their role as prophets and "read the signs of the times." These signs revolve around the terrorist attacks of September 11, 2001, and the subsequent wars in Afghanistan and Iraq. A vicious circle of violence has broken out. "In the midst of a world where it is extremely difficult to break the chain of violence," the bishops said, "let us do everything we can to spread the spirit and practice of nonviolence, to construct a new solidarity with the people of the world on the common issues, and thus strive for peace." Though Christians are but a small fraction of Japan's 128 million people, their presence is noted, perhaps chiefly because it was the Christian district of Urakami in Nagasaki that bore the brunt of the atomic attack on that city. About 8,500 of the 12,000 parishioners at Urakami Cathedral, at that time the largest in Asia, were estimated to have died in the bombing. Out of the wasteland of Nagasaki and Hiroshima has come a seeming rebirth of the human spirit.

Mayors for Peace Campaign

No person better symbolizes the transformation of Hiroshima from a city of death to a city of life than its mayor, Tadatoshi Akiba. He is a most unusual Japanese politician, for he spent nearly 20 years in the United States before returning to his homeland. Following his university work in mathematics in Tokyo, Akiba went to the U.S. in 1968 and earned a PhD at the Massachusetts Institute of Technology; his field was topology, the study of the properties of geometric figures or solids. He taught at Tufts University in Boston from 1972 to 1986. He returned to Japan to become a visiting professor of humanities at Hiroshima University and, in 1990, was elected to Japan's House of Representatives. In 1999, he was elected mayor of Hiroshima and has come into world prominence for his work developing the organization Mayors for Peace.

When the atomic bombs fell on Hiroshima and Nagasaki, Akiba was three years old and living outside Tokyo. He once said, "The longest minute I ever experienced was the time I was waiting for my mother to come back from our bomb shelter where she carried my baby brother when the air raid warning sounded. Later, when I learned what had happened to Hiroshima and Nagasaki, it was very natural that those experiences merged with mine to form my basic feelings about war and human suffering." While a faculty member at Tufts, Akiba became an activist, sparked by listening to a Boston radio call-in show discussing whether America's use of the atomic bomb was right or wrong. To his dismay, 90 per cent of the callers said the bombing was justified. Akiba believed it was important to explain the implications of such violence and the long-term effects an atomic bomb has on both the physical and mental health of the survivors.

Although running Hiroshima demands that much of his time be spent on environment, economic and information technology issues, Akiba has also concentrated on reviving Mayors for Peace. The organization, begun in the 1980s, had lapsed somewhat by the time Akiba came to office. He determined to make it a leading force in the drive to build world public opinion against nuclear weapons. He has quadrupled the membership to 1,080 mayors in 112 countries and hired a veteran peace activist, Aaron Tovish, to double that number.

Akiba launched the Vision 2020 Campaign, which he calls an emergency campaign to eliminate all nuclear weapons by the year 2020, the 75th anniversary of the atomic bombings of Hiroshima and Nagasaki. Neither Akiba himself nor any mayor can do this alone; this speaks directly to the core of the problem. It is national governments that control nuclear weapons and the attendant policies, not municipalities. For the most part, these "senior" governments do not like their junior partners meddling in the big issues. This is certainly true of Japan, whose national government, heavily influenced by U.S. policies, treats local mayors as almost non-existent. But, gradually, mayors in many parts of the world are beginning to assert their legitimate interest in keeping their hospital, transportation, food, water and sanitation systems from being blown to pieces. In other words, cities would be on the front lines of nuclear warfare and have a right to speak out against nuclear weapons. As one mayor put it, "It is the cities that bombs will fall on, not national governments."

It is in the U.S., perhaps ironically, considering the government's pro-nuclear stand, where mayors have spoken out most strongly. In 2004, the United States Conference of

Mayors, which represents more than 1,000 of America's largest cities, passed a resolution declaring that "weapons of mass destruction have no place in a civilized world" and called for the immediate commencement of negotiations to prohibit and eliminate nuclear weapons; the negotiations should be concluded in 2010 and fully implemented by 2020. Akiba reasons that when enough mayors around the world start putting pressure on governments, action will follow.

Some 50 mayors and representatives from nineteen countries joined a contingent of their Japanese colleagues for a three-day Mayors for Peace Conference to launch the 60th anniversary observance. Before the conference began, I went to see Akiba in his office at city hall. I have known him for several years and, in 2004, accompanied him on his visit to a number of Canadian cities. I found him quite serene in the midst of a bustling office. "I spent the morning in the Peace Museum," I told him. "And the message I got was as much about the future as the past. Was that the message you wanted me to get?" Akiba, dressed in an open-necked shirt with navy jacket and tan trousers, looked at me intently. "Yes," he said. "A consideration for our children and the lives they will face should determine our present action. The message the *hibakusha* give us from the past is that no one else should suffer as they did, but also that the children of today and to come should not be killed by nuclear weapons." The *hibakusha* are teaching us reconciliation, he said, and that must be forward-minded.

We spoke about the work of Mayors for Peace to build public opinion. "The mayors teach us that this is not just some abstract subject for government theoreticians," he said. "Nuclear weapons can wipe out humanity. Mayors understand that." Because they are practical politicians, close to the people, he added, mayors can cut through the spurious arguments given by government defenders of nuclear weapons. Akiba concluded by saying that the advocates for the elimination of nuclear weapons are now in the majority around the world. Mayors can activate that majority.

The Mayors for Peace Conference took up Akiba's theme of pressing governments to start negotiating a treaty to abolish nuclear weapons by 2020. The group added a note of its own: "Invite government leaders, in particular those of countries possessing nuclear weapons, to visit Hiroshima and Nagasaki to see with their own eyes what nuclear weapons have in store for them."

Akiba's leadership is vital to the success of Mayors for Peace. He has the stature, combined with an effective speaking style and superb command of English, to make an impact on governments. But he also has right-wing critics at home who would like nothing better than to unseat him in the next election. Akiba is one of those Japanese leaders standing in the way of a drive in Japan to overturn Article 9 of the constitution, sometimes known as the pacifist clause. It reads: "Aspiring sincerely to an international peace based on justice and order, the Japanese people forever renounce war as a sovereign right of the nation and the threat or use of force as means of settling international disputes.... [L]and, sea, air forces, as well as other war potential, will never be retained. The right of belligerency of the state will not be recognized." The Japanese government has always interpreted this article to mean that the nation can possess armed forces only for self-defence. But some in the ruling Liberal Democratic Party believe that Japan must militarize to maintain security in the face of international terrorism and a nuclear-armed North Korea. Others want to protect the constitution on the grounds that renouncing Article 9 would send a message to its neighbours that Japan is once again considering war. The U.S. Administration has been pressing Tokyo for the change and the debate is gathering strength in Japan. One of the effects of renunciation, should it occur, would be to open up the possibility of Japan acquiring nuclear weapons.

Akiba took the occasion of the City of Hiroshima's annual Peace Declaration to speak up for retaining Article 9, built on the axiom of peace, as "a guiding light for the world in the 21st century." In the Declaration, he went on to excoriate the U.S., Russia, the U.K., France, China, India, Pakistan and North Korea for "ignoring the majority voices of the people…":

> Based on the dogma, "might is right," these countries have formed their own 'nuclear club,' the admission requirement being the possession of nuclear weapons. Through the media, they have long repeated the incantation, 'nuclear weapons protect you.' With no means of rebuttal, many people worldwide have succumbed to the feeling that 'There is nothing we can do.' Within the United Nations, nuclear club members use their veto power to override the global majority and pursue their selfish interests.

Though more attention is paid globally to Hiroshima, the feelings in Nagasaki are the same. Mayor Iccho Itoh, who was born just two weeks after the bombing there, is highly critical of the nuclear weapons states' retention of their deadly arsenals. Addressing the Nagasaki 60th observance ceremonies, he said he understood the U.S. anger over the September 11 terrorist attacks. "Yet is your security enhanced by your…policies of maintaining 10,000 nuclear weapons, of carrying out repeated sub-critical nuclear tests, and of pursuing the development of new 'mini' nuclear weapons?" He called on Japan to end its dependence on the U.S. nuclear umbrella in the face of uneasy relations with China and North Korea.

The relationship with the U.S. continues to be the centrepiece of Japanese foreign policy. The strong desire for approbation from Washington has Japan walking on a tightrope. Hiroshima and Nagasaki give Japan the moral standing to lead the world in the struggle to abolish nuclear weapons.

Operational Nuclear Weapons (2005)

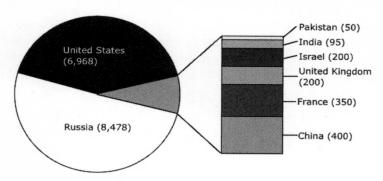

The number of operational strategic and tactical nuclear weapons shown above totals 16,741. In addition, Russia has up to 11,000 nuclear weapons in storage, and the U.S., an additional 3,000. Thus, there are at least 30,741 nuclear weapons in existence. Some estimates are higher because analysts do not agree on the precise numbers. Governments hold nuclear weapons information in secret. The essential point is this: the known nuclear arsenals have a destructive power hundreds of thousands of times greater than that of the bombs that destroyed Hiroshima and Nagasaki. The conduct of the nuclear powers is in stark contrast to what all 188 states parties to the Non-Proliferation Treaty agreed to in 2000, as shown below.

Sources: *Arms Control Association, Carnegie Endowment for International Peace, Congressional Research Service, Institute for Science and International Security, International Atomic Energy Agency, and Natural Resources Defense Council.*

"The total elimination of nuclear weapons is the only absolute guarantee against the use or threat of use of nuclear weapons."

Final Document, 2000 NPT Review Conference

But this attachment to the U.S. holds the country back. Mayor Akiba's hope of reinvigorating Japan with policies for peace requires pressure on the government from outside of which Mayors for Peace is now capable.

I left Hiroshima pondering its lesson. Though it symbolizes a tragic moment of the past, the city is not trapped in its history. It is vibrant with life, as if to say that the sting of death cannot destroy the spirit. Hiroshima has lived to give its testimony to the world. It has the moral stature to say to the world: No more nuclear weapons. Hiroshima proclaims this message softly; some sensitivity is required to hear it. The last photo in the Peace Museum exhibit makes the point gently. It shows a flower blooming in the scorched earth. The inscription says:

That autumn in Hiroshima where it was said,
"For 75 years, nothing will grow,"
New buds sprouted
In the green that came back to life.
Among the charred ruins
People recovered
Their living hopes and courage.

2

The Bargain and the Promises

On Sunday morning, May 1, 2005, Hiroshima mayor Akiba and his colleague Mayor Iccoh Itoh of Nagasaki took their places in the front row of marchers gathering on First Avenue in New York, two blocks from the United Nations headquarters, for a rally to protest against nuclear weapons. Thousands of peace activists, many from Japan, surrounded them as they set off towards 42nd Street, over to Sixth Avenue, then up through Manhattan to Central Park. "Abolish all nuclear weapons," the banners proclaimed. "Let there be no more Hiroshimas and no more Nagasakis!"

The marchers were guarded every step of the way by New York police, but it was hard to tell why, unless senior politicians had decided that peace marchers are inherently dangerous in a time of war. That the United States is at war – an unending war against terrorism – has become a constant refrain in the country's political rhetoric and in the media. The mood of the march was buoyant, with songs and chants keeping it lighthearted. Still, the idea of the police heavily guarding peace marchers, who want nothing so much as to express sentiments of love and hope rather than fire off Molotov cocktails, seems jolting in a society founded on freedom.

The presence of police in such massive numbers testifies to the palpable fear that permeates big city life in the post-

9/11 age. It is this fear, mixed with denial and dominance, that is working against the abolition of nuclear weapons. Twenty-three years earlier, in 1982, a similar march through the streets of New York calling for nuclear sanity drew one million protesters. This was at the peak of the Cold War, with the U.S. and the Soviet Union threatening each other with ever-new nuclear weapons systems. Nevertheless, the atmosphere of that march did not seem as threatening to establishment values as the 2005 version did, with only 40,000 marchers, at most. But since anti-globalization protests of recent years have turned ugly, susceptible as they are to anarchist penetration, the police (perhaps more so the politicians) are understandably anxious. This time they had no need to worry.

The marchers entered the Heckscher ball field of Central Park and formed a peace symbol to be photographed from a helicopter. The organizers, United for Peace and Justice, and Abolition Now!, brought a dozen speakers to the microphone to protest the Iraq war, nuclear weapons and social injustices while the crowd sat on the lawns and in bleachers. The day was sunny and hot. Children ran around. Ice cream vendors flourished. People seemed to be having a good time, despite the subject matter.

The contrast between this peaceful setting and U.N. Secretary-General Kofi Annan's opening words the next morning to the Review Conference of the Non-Proliferation Treaty (NPT) was startling: "Imagine just for a minute," he told the delegates who had gathered at the United Nations from around the world, the consequences of a nuclear catastrophe for one of the great cities of the world.

> Tens, if not hundreds, of thousands of people would perish in an instant, and many more would die from exposure to radiation.... World financial markets, trade and transportation would be hard hit, with major economic consequences. This could drive

millions of people in poor countries into deeper deprivation and suffering.

One minute, people are sitting in a park in a great city, refreshing themselves away from the urban density; the next, they have been blown apart or left victims in agonizing chaos. That is the essential framework of knowledge needed to understand the crisis of nuclear weapons today. We just do not know when our world of ever-expanding development, security and human rights could, as Annan says, be put irrevocably beyond our reach by a nuclear explosion.

The Sunday marchers had come to energize the diplomats. Kofi Annan tried to jolt them. An exhibit mounted by the cities of Hiroshima and Nagasaki in the lobby of the U.N. building spoke to their consciences. Photos of the devastated cities were shown. Underneath were these words:

Raise your eyes,
Friends!
Look at the hidden truth
The horror of nuclear weapons.

The Bargain of 1968

In the mid-1960s, when the nuclear arms race was accelerating and disarmament negotiations were overpowered by the intensity of the Cold War, a round of diplomatic discussions started, aimed at stopping the spread of nuclear weapons. Already, the United Kingdom, France and China had joined the nuclear club, whose pioneer members were the U.S. and the Soviet Union. President John F. Kennedy, shortly before his assassination, warned that, if the international community did not stop the proliferation of nuclear weapons, some 20 states would have them in a few years. By 1968, the NPT had been successfully negotiated, and it came into force in 1970. A bargain was struck between the nuclear and non-nuclear states. The former agreed to negotiate in good faith the elimination of their nuclear weapons in return for the latter not acquiring nuclear weapons while still receiving access to nuclear energy. Two principles underlie the NPT. The first is that the spread of nuclear weapons undermines international peace and security. The second is that the peaceful application of nuclear energy should be universally available. Since the nuclear age began after the signing of the U.N. charter, the NPT actually supplements the charter in addressing the problems of the atom.

The NPT involves five commitments: acceptance of a political and moral norm against the possession of nuclear weapons, the obligation to eliminate existing stocks of weapons, international co-operation in the peaceful uses of nuclear energy, special assistance to developing countries, and measures to ensure a world free of nuclear weapons. In essence, the NPT promised a world in which nuclear weapons would be eliminated and technological co-operation for development of peaceful uses for nuclear energy would be widespread.

The NPT certainly did not bless the existence of nuclear weapons. It simply accepted the basic fact that the U.S., Soviet Union, U.K., France and China possessed them. The five countries signed the NPT as nuclear weapons states (NWS). All other states would join as non–nuclear weapons states (NNWS).

Here is what the NPT says.

Under Article I, NWS agree to refrain from transferring nuclear weapons to any recipient. Similarly, under Article II, NNWS undertake not to receive or control any nuclear weapons.

Article III obliges NNWS to accept the safeguards of the International Atomic Energy Agency "with a view to preventing diversion of nuclear energy from peaceful uses to nuclear weapons or other nuclear explosive devices." Both NWS and NNWS must refrain from providing fissionable and related material to any NNWS, unless it is safeguarded.

Article IV emphasizes the universal right to the development of nuclear energy for peaceful purposes and the need for co-operation, "with the consideration for the needs of the developing areas of the world." Article V reinforces the peaceful application benefits to NNWS from any nuclear explosions by NWS. Since all states have observed a moratorium on nuclear test explosions for the past few years, this article has become moot.

The centrepiece of the NPT is Article VI, which states in its entirety:

> Each of the Parties to the Treaty undertakes to pursue negotiations in good faith on effective measures relating to cessation of the nuclear arms race at an early date and to nuclear disarmament, and on a treaty on general and complete disarmament under strict and effective international control.

This language explicates the spirit of the NPT's preamble, which speaks of the need to ease international tensions to facilitate the cessation of nuclear weapons production and the elimination of weapons and delivery systems from national arsenals. The preamble adds that, in accordance with the U.N. Charter, countries must refrain from the threat or use of force; international peace and security are to be promoted "with the least diversion for armaments of the world's human and economic resources."

Although references to Article VI frequently relate to the obligations of the NWS, the text actually addresses all parties. It is clearly the language of compromise. The continuing battle over the efficacy of the NPT centres on the interpretation of the language. Many NNWS argue that the primary obligation of the NPT belongs to the NWS to get rid of nuclear weapons, an act that would be instrumental to advancing general disarmament. For their part, the NWS hold that they have stopped the nuclear arms race and that further progress towards eliminating nuclear weapons is contingent on the easing of international tensions. The International Court of Justice ruled in its landmark advisory opinion of 1996, however, that nuclear disarmament is not conditional on general and complete disarmament. Moreover, the Court said, states have an obligation to *conclude* nuclear disarmament negotiations.

Article VII promotes nuclear weapons–free zones, geographic areas in which all the states have declared themselves free of nuclear weapons. There are four such zones: Latin America and the Caribbean, the South Pacific, Southeast Asia, and Africa.

Article VIII provides for a five-year review of the NPT. Article IX sets up the ratification process. Article X allows a state to withdraw from the NPT on three months' notice when it decides that extraordinary events "have jeopardized the supreme interests of its country." Article XI establishes the United States, the United Kingdom and the Soviet Union as the three depository states.

The Promises of 1995 and 2000

In 1995, the original 25-year term of the NPT was indefinitely extended. The nuclear weapons states committed themselves to "systematic and progressive efforts to reduce nuclear weapons globally, with the ultimate goal of eliminating those weapons," and all states pledged to pursue "general and complete disarmament under strict and effective international control." In addition, all states promised to complete the Comprehensive Nuclear Test Ban Treaty by 1996 and to bring to an "early conclusion" negotiations for a treaty banning the production of fissile material for nuclear weapons. The 1995 promises were augmented at the 2000 NPT Review Conference when the nuclear weapons states joined a consensus on an "unequivocal undertaking" for the complete elimination of nuclear weapons to be carried out through thirteen practical steps.

Summary of the Thirteen Practical Steps for Nuclear Disarmament

1. Achieve early entry-into-force of the Comprehensive Test Ban Treaty.
2. Implement a moratorium on nuclear testing pending entry-into-force of the test ban treaty.
3. Conclude negotiations for a fissile materials treaty.
4. Establish a subsidiary body to the Conference on Disarmament to deal with nuclear disarmament.
5. Confirm the principle of irreversibility of nuclear disarmament.
6. Unequivocally undertake to completely eliminate nuclear arsenals.
7. Achieve early entry-into-force of START II, conclude START III and preserve and strengthen the Anti-Ballistic Missile Treaty.
8. Complete and implement the Trilateral Initiative between the United States, Russia and the International Atomic Energy Agency.
9. Take steps toward nuclear disarmament in a way that promotes international stability, based on the principle of undiminished security for all:
   - unilateral reduction;
   - increased transparency;
   - further reduction of non-strategic nuclear weapons;
   - de-alerting of nuclear weapons systems;
   - diminished role for nuclear weapons in security policies; and
   - engagement of all nuclear weapons states as soon as is appropriate.
10. Arrange for nuclear weapons states to place the fissile material they no longer require for military purposes under the auspices of the International Atomic Energy Agency or other international body for verification.
11. Reaffirm the ultimate object of general and complete disarmament under effective international control.
12. Make regular reports, within the Non-Proliferation Treaty's strengthened review process.
13. Further develop verification capabilities.

The Thirteen Steps included such measures as the following:

• *Achieve early entry-into-force of the Comprehensive Test Ban Treaty.* This treaty was negotiated and opened for signature in 1996, and 175 states have signed it, but before it becomes operable it must be ratified by the 44 countries that have nuclear reactors. By 2005, only 33 had done so. The chief holdout is the United States. Although President Bill Clinton was the first to sign the treaty in 1996, the U.S. Senate rejected it for reasons that had as much to do with domestic policy as nuclear weapons. When the Bush administration came to power, the U.S. withdrew its support for the treaty, and took steps to re-activate test sites, although it is currently respecting a moratorium on testing. China is the only other major requisite holdout, but has said that ratification is working its way through the parliamentary process.

• *Conclude negotiation on a multilateral and verifiable treaty banning the production of fissile material for nuclear weapons.* The Conference on Disarmament, a permanent 66-nation body in Geneva that is supposed to host these negotiations, has been paralyzed for a decade because issues keep getting inter-linked. The Conference operates by consensus, meaning that any one country can exercise a virtual veto, and this happens continually.

• *Establish a subsidiary body to the Conference on Disarmament to deal with nuclear disarmament.* There has been no action on this.

• *Confirm the principle of irreversibility of nuclear disarmament.* This step would ensure that the reduction process could not be reversed. The nuclear weapons states are ignoring this and are modernizing their nuclear arsenals. The Moscow Treaty of 2002, in which the U.S. and Russia undertook to reduce their strategic nuclear weapons to between 1,700 and 2,200 by 2012, does not actually provide for the destruction of the warheads or delivery systems, even though they would be removed from deployment.

• *Unequivocally undertake to completely eliminate nuclear arsenals.* None of the nuclear weapons states has removed the option to produce nuclear weapons; most have refused to enter into comprehensive negotiations for elimination.

• *Preserve and strengthen the Anti-Ballistic Missile (ABM) Treaty.* The treaty, which the U.S. and the Soviet Union entered into in 1972, prohibited national missile defences. It was recognized at the time that such defence systems only serve to spur the development of new offensive weapons. But the Bush administration, determined to implement a missile defence system, abrogated the treaty and it is now dead.

• *Take steps towards nuclear disarmament in a way that promotes international stability, based on the principle of undiminished security for all.* This commitment is full of diplomatic ambiguities. It allows nuclear weapons states to argue that taking some specific steps, such as reducing the operational status of nuclear weapons systems, is not in their security interests. As long as the nuclear powers continue to claim that nuclear weapons are necessary for their "undiminished security," not much progress towards implementing the "unequivocal undertaking" will occur.

• *Reaffirm the ultimate objective of general and complete disarmament under effective international control.* The nuclear weapons states have continued to argue that nuclear disarmament can only occur when there is a greater degree of peace in various regions; the non–nuclear states hold that nuclear weapons are inherently destabilizing and must be eliminated in the process of reducing all stocks of armaments.

Some nuclear weapons states are now claiming that the Thirteen Steps were merely political commitments and are now outdated. But the U.S.-based Lawyers' Committee on Nuclear Policy holds that these steps have the force of law because they fulfill the legal obligations set out in Article VI of the NPT. Because the 2000 NPT Review Conference agreed by consensus on these systematic and progressive efforts to implement Article VI, the Thirteen Steps became inextricably bound up in the disarmament process. This legal basis of the Thirteen Steps thus obliges states to achieve the complete elimination of nuclear weapons without any precondition of comprehensive demilitarization.

Nonetheless, when preparation for the 2005 NPT Review started in 2002, it was clear that the commitments of 1995 and 2000 were crumbling. The U.S. announced that it "no longer supports" some of the steps. It stepped up plans for a new "bunker-buster" nuclear weapon, and has only been slowed by congressional resistance to funding. North Korea, in the process of developing a nuclear weapon, withdrew from the NPT. Iran came under attack for allegedly preparing to divert to weapons nuclear materials obtained under the peaceful use provisions of the Treaty. Libya revealed that it had been developing a nuclear weapon but gave it up to get back into the good graces of the big powers. Mayor Akiba has often warned, "We stand today on the brink of hyper-proliferation and perhaps of repeating the third use of nuclear weapons."

A Two-Class World Becoming Permanent

All these issues came to a head when the U.S. claimed that NPT priority should be to stop the proliferation of nuclear weapons and that there was no problem with their own compliance with Article VI – good faith negotiation towards the complete elimination of nuclear weapons. The leading non-nuclear weapons states claimed exactly the opposite: the proliferation of nuclear weapons cannot be stopped while the nuclear weapons states arrogate to themselves the possession of nuclear weapons and refuse to enter into comprehensive negotiations to eliminate them, as directed by the International Court of Justice.

When the U.S., aided by its Western nuclear partners, the U.K. and France, tried to shift the focus away from nuclear disarmament to stopping proliferation, all trust broke down. Brazil tartly observed: "One cannot worship at the altar of nuclear weapons and raise heresy charges against those who want to join the sect." The whole international community, nuclear and non-nuclear alike, is concerned about proliferation, but the new attempt by the nuclear weapons states to gloss over the discriminatory aspects of the NPT, which are now becoming permanent, has snapped the patience of many members of the 119-state Non-Aligned Movement. They see a two-class world of nuclear haves and have-nots becoming a permanent feature of the global landscape. In such chaos, the NPT is eroding, and the prospect looms once more of the number of nuclear weapons states multiplying, a fear that caused nations to produce the NPT in the first place. The U.N. High-Level Panel on Threats, Challenges and Change put the danger graphically: "We are approaching a point at which the erosion of the non-proliferation regime could become irreversible and result in a cascade of proliferation."

By the time the 2005 NPT Review Conference opened, the mood had turned sour. Preparatory meetings had ended in disarray, with countries unable even to agree on an agenda. The U.S., claiming that the terrorist attacks of 9/11 had brought about a new world, refused to allow any references to the commitments of 1995 and 2000. This attempt at revisionist history shocked even the American allies and drew the ire of the Non-Aligned Movement, particularly Egypt and Iran, which refused to co-operate to tighten regulations to prevent any party to the NPT from using its access to nuclear materials to divert such materials to nuclear weapons.

When he went to the podium in the U.N. General Assembly to open the Review Conference, Secretary-General Annan named the issue squarely. "Some will paint proliferation as a grave threat," he said. "Others will argue that *existing* nuclear arsenals are a deadly danger." Thus, he challenged delegates to recognize the truth that disarmament, non-proliferation and the right to peaceful uses of nuclear energy are all vital and must not be held hostage to the politics of the past. Annan warned that the gap between the promise and the performance of the non-proliferation regime may become unbridgeable without "bold decisions." He called for prompt negotiation of a fissile material treaty, maintenance of the moratorium on nuclear testing, early entry-into-force of the Comprehensive Test Ban Treaty, de-alerted strategic nuclear weapons, and assurances for non-nuclear weapons states that they will not be attacked by nuclear states. States living under a nuclear umbrella (e.g., NATO) must overcome their reliance on nuclear deterrence.

The Secretary-General was immediately followed by Mohamed ElBaradei, Director General of the International Atomic Energy Agency (IAEA), the closest entity the NPT has for a watchdog. The IAEA's team of 2,200 professional and support staff carries out safeguards inspections under legal agreement with states to verify the exclusively peaceful nature of nuclear material and activities, applies safety and security standards, and provides technical assistance for nuclear applications in health, agriculture and related fields. ElBaradei also pointed to the increasing dangers since the 2000 Review Conference:

> In five years, the world has changed. Our fears of a deadly nuclear detonation – whatever the cause – have been reawakened. In part, these fears are driven by new realities. The rise in terrorism. The discovery of clandestine nuclear programmes. The emergence of a nuclear black market.

ElBaradei emphasized that as long as some countries rely on nuclear weapons as a strategic deterrent, other countries will emulate them. "We cannot delude ourselves into thinking otherwise."

The Record of the Nuclear Weapons States

As they came to the podium for their own turn in the general debate, the leaders of the nuclear weapons states appeared not to have even heard the warnings of Annan and ElBaradei. One by one, the U.S., Russia, the U.K., France and China trumpeted their good work to reduce the stocks of nuclear weaponry while completely ignoring the core of the Article VI commitment: negotiations for the elimination of nuclear weapons. Hamid Albar, Foreign Affairs Minister of Malaysia and Chairman of the Non-Aligned Movement, criticized the nuclear weapons states for modernizing their nuclear arsenals, unravelling the NPT and threatening international peace and security.

What is it that the nuclear weapons states are doing that so concerns their critics?

The United States is modifying existing nuclear warheads to achieve additional capabilities. The Bush administration requested $8.5 million for research on modifying the high-yield B-83 bomb to test the feasibility of creating a new Nuclear Earth Penetrator ("bunker-buster") and has said another $14 million will be needed to complete the research in 2007. The program is controversial and opponents in Congress are trying to block funding, but the government presses on. It is retooling the nuclear weapons research, design and production infrastructure to maintain a nuclear arsenal still numbering in the thousands of weapons for many decades to come. The U.S. is spending $40 billion annually on all its nuclear forces, more than the total military budget of almost all other countries. Seeking even more funding, the Bush administration plans to rebuild every weapon in the U.S. stockpile and install new components to make weapons lighter, more rugged, and more resistant to radiation, to improve the consistency of their explosive yield, and to improve the accuracy of delivery.

On November 17, 2004, President Vladimir Putin of Russia confirmed that his country is "carrying out research and missile tests of state-of-the-art nuclear missile systems" and that Russia would "continue to build up firmly and insistently our armed forces, including the nuclear component." Later, Russia's defence minister, Sergei Ivanov, announced that Moscow will soon have a unique new generation of nuclear weapons "not possessed by any country in the world." Other Russian officials have touted the development of a new maneuverable warhead able to avoid missile defences. President Putin described it as a "new hypersound-speed, high-precision new weapons system that can hit targets at international distance and can adjust their altitude and course as they travel." Manufacture of single-warhead, silo-based missiles continues. The deployment of a road-based multi-warhead is scheduled to begin in 2006. Russia has announced it will eventually field several divisions of these missiles, likely totalling about 200 missiles, of which 40 have already been completed and deployed. Russia continues to slowly retire multi-warhead, land-based nuclear missiles, but may deploy recent variants while building up the number of single warhead missiles. Reportedly, development of a new generation intercontinental ballistic missile (ICBM), able to carry up to 10 warheads, is under way. A nuclear variant of a new bomber-carried cruise missile may be deployed in 2005. When ready and flight-tested, a new submarine-launched missile will be deployed on two submarines under construction.

The United Kingdom stands on the edge of an historic decision. The submarine-launched Trident missile, equipped with three or four warheads, is Britain's remaining operational nuclear weapons system. A decision on whether to replace the aging system is soon to be made. Should Britain decide not to replace the Trident system, the country would earn a special place in history as the first of the NPT nuclear weapons states to renounce its arsenal. Meanwhile, officials are saying that Britain's aim is in part to "maintain a capability to provide warheads for a successor system" to the Trident without "recourse to nuclear testing."

In 2001, President Jacques Chirac of France said his nation's security "is now and will be guaranteed above all by our nuclear deterrent;" France's status as a nuclear weapons state is guaranteed for many years. For its submarine fleet, France is developing the M-51 missile, which will eventually be equipped with a new warhead, the *Tête nucléaire océanique*. Modernization of the air-to-surface stocks continues with the current cruise missile set to be replaced with a longer range variant, also equipped with a new warhead, the *Tête nucléaire aéroportée.* France has a highly advanced program to develop the capability to design and manufacture modified or new nuclear weapons without explosive nuclear testing. Notably, with the Laser Megajoule now under construction, France is the only state, other than the United States, seeking to induce miniature thermonuclear explosions in contained vessels in giant laser facilities.

China is currently replacing its force of 20 silo-based long-range missiles with a longer range variant. China is also developing a new mobile intermediate-range solid-fuel ICBM, which the country may begin to deploy by the end of the decade. A longer range variant is also under development. China is currently working to replace its experimental submarine-based missile with a more reliable, medium-range missile, and is developing a new submarine. The Chinese nuclear program could be characterized as a slow-motion effort to counterbalance long-standing and still evolving U.S. and Russian capabilities. Nonetheless, its activities are a form of arms racing.

Standing outside the NPT, India has an estimated 95 nuclear weapons, Pakistan 50, and Israel 200. All are engaged in modernization. The eight countries now in the nuclear club have a combined population of 3.1 billion, which means that 48 per cent of the people in the world live in a nuclear weapons state. The small to mid-level states are increasingly resisting this nuclear hegemony.

The United States: Key to the Future

Are nuclear weapons to become the currency of power in the 21st century should the major states not give them up? The actions of the United States are the key to answering that question. If the U.S. became active in pursuing the Thirteen Steps to nuclear disarmament, there is no doubt that Russia, the U.K. and France would follow. China has already said it wants to move in this direction. The smaller nuclear states would not be able to resist a U.S.-led world-wide movement to fully implement the NPT without discrimination.

The U.S. possesses the most powerful military forces in the history of the world. Moreover, it is the linchpin of NATO, which is an expanding Western military alliance.

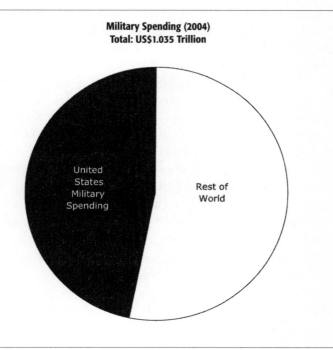

Military Spending (2004)
Total: US$1.035 Trillion

United States Military Spending

Rest of World

Source: Stockholm International Peace Research Institute

Pentagon documents speak of the necessity of the U.S. maintaining "full spectrum dominance" – dominance in the air, on land, in the sea and in space. Thus, when the U.S. asserted in its 2001 Nuclear Posture Review that it requires nuclear weapons to "assure allies and friends," "dissuade competitors," "deter aggressors" and "defeat enemies," it lost all credibility in its parallel assertions that it is in full compliance with Article VI of the NPT. The Nuclear Posture Review, citing U.S. plans to revitalize its nuclear forces, shows indisputably that nuclear weapons remain a cornerstone of U.S. national security policy.

This policy was directly attacked by Robert McNamara, former U.S. Secretary of Defense in the Kennedy and Johnson administrations, who spoke at a noon-hour meeting during the Review Conference. Now 88, McNamara has become an outspoken critic of nuclear weapons in his later years. He wrote an article for *Foreign Policy*, published by the prestigious Carnegie Endowment for International Peace, which was prominently displayed on the literature tables. The cover arrested the attention of delegates. It showed a mushroom cloud with the title of the lead article superimposed: "Apocalypse Soon: Why American Nukes Are Immoral, Illegal and Dreadfully Dangerous."

McNamara appeared on a panel sponsored by the Global Security Institute, a U.S.-based non-governmental organization, with Ted Sorensen, former special counsel to President John F. Kennedy, and Ambassador Thomas Graham, who led the U.S. delegation to the 1995 NPT Review and Extension Conference. Both were also highly critical of U.S. policy. McNamara repeated his characterization of current U.S. nuclear weapons policy as "immoral, illegal, militarily unnecessary, and dreadfully dangerous." Because 2,000 of the 8,000 active or operational U.S. warheads are on hair-trigger alert, ready to be launched on 15 minutes' warning, "the risk of an accidental or inadvertent nuclear launch is unacceptably high."

The average U.S. warhead, he says, has a destructive power 20 times that of the Hiroshima bomb. But far from reducing these risks, the Bush administration is keeping the U.S. nuclear arsenal as a mainstay of its military power. It refuses to ask the Senate to ratify the Comprehensive Nuclear Test Ban Treaty, has ordered the national laboratories to begin research on new nuclear weapons, and is preparing underground test sites in Nevada for nuclear tests. In short, the Bush administration assumes that nuclear weapons will be part of U.S. military forces for at least the next several decades. In his speech, McNamara scorned U.S. policy:

> The statement that our nuclear weapons do not target populations per se was and remains totally misleading in the sense that the so-called collateral damage of large nuclear strikes would include tens of millions of innocent civilian dead.
>
> … This in a nutshell is what nuclear weapons do: they indiscriminately blast, burn, and irradiate with a speed and finality that are almost incomprehensible. This is exactly what countries like the United States and Russia, with nuclear weapons on hair-trigger alert, continue to threaten every minute of every day in this new 21st century.

How does the U.S. answer these charges? The U.S. delegation distributed several glossy brochures and pamphlets (omitting any reference to the 2000 NPT commitments and test ban treaty), which made the point that when the Moscow Treaty is fully implemented in 2012, the U.S. will have reduced the number of strategic nuclear warheads it deployed in 1990 by 80 per cent. In addition, non-strategic (i.e. tactical or short-range) nuclear weapons have been reduced by 90 per cent since the end of the Cold War.

Since 1997, the U.S. says it has done the following:

• eliminated 64 heavy bombers by chopping them into pieces;

• eliminated 150 ICBM silos by destroying or dismantling them;

• taken out of strategic service four ballistic missile submarines by removing the missiles and modifying the submarines so that they can no longer carry such missiles; and

• retired and removed 37 Peacekeeper ICBMs from silos by January 2005, with the remaining 13 scheduled for deactivation by October 2005.

These systems are not being replaced. U.S. defence spending on strategic nuclear forces has declined from seven per cent of the defense department's budget during the Cold War to less than three per cent today. In the last fifteen years, the United States has terminated a number of strategic nuclear weapons modernization programs, including the mobile ICBM program, and limited the production of the B-2 heavy bomber.

The U.S. says it does not target any country with nuclear weapons, its strategic bombers are no longer on alert and it is not developing, testing or producing nuclear warheads. It does concede that it is doing "modest" research on advanced nuclear weapon concepts and a study on adapting an existing nuclear weapon to strike hardened, deeply buried targets. But it insists that the robust Nuclear Earth Penetrator is only intended to enhance deterrence using an existing warhead. "It should also be remembered that nuclear weapons modernization by nuclear weapons states is not prohibited under the NPT." The U.S. denies that new low-yield nuclear weapons would lower the nuclear threshold. Moreover, it says, the assertion that current U.S. policy is driving North Korea and Iran nuclear weapons is not based on any evidence. "The programs of these states and others that have violated their non-proliferation obligations predate current U.S. policy. Would they stop even if the United States completely disarmed?" Also, the U.S. says it has no plans to conduct nuclear tests. Its enhanced test readiness program, designed to reduce the time required to undertake a nuclear test, is to provide "appropriate capabilities for, and training of, future stewards of the stockpile": improving nuclear systems does not presume future decisions but ensures that as long as the U.S. possesses nuclear weapons it "will have the capability to deal with them safely and responsibly."

In summation, the U.S. sees itself as being the world leader in realizing Article VI objectives through deep reductions in nuclear forces. "The U.S. continues to be a leader in these areas and on many other fronts in support of the NPT":

> There can be no artificial timetables for progress in realizing our common Article VI objectives. Details and dates cannot and should not be predicted or foreordained. Attempts to do so would not advance, and might undermine, expected progress in arms reductions and disarmament. Instead, progress will depend on the broader international context, including success in promoting regional and international peace and security. U.S. efforts to ensure compliance with NPT and other undertakings are critical contributions to this end, as are other efforts to strengthen the Treaty, International Atomic Energy Agency (IAEA) safeguards and export controls.

The U.S. draws some comfort for its strategy from the Carnegie Endowment for International Peace, which distributed its publication, *Universal Compliance: A Strategy for Nuclear Security*. It said the twin goals of U.S. nuclear policy should be to prevent new actors from acquiring nuclear weapons and to reduce towards zero the risk that those who have these weapons will use them. The organization maintains that non-proliferation objectives should drive nuclear policy – and that is exactly what is happening. The U.S. deterrent, for its part, backs up security guarantees to protect important allies such as Japan, South Korea and Germany. In the Carnegie Endowment's view, relying on U.S. security guarantees lessens these countries' interest in acquiring nuclear weapons themselves:

> Thus, the United States must maintain an effective, reliable nuclear deterrent for as long as nuclear threats remain in the world, even as it pursues a

vigorous non-proliferation strategy. The question for the U.S. policy-makers is how best to pursue these two critical goals…. Two radically different approaches have been advanced: to acquire new nuclear weapons with more useable characteristics, thus to dissuade proliferation; and to de-emphasize and devalue nuclear weapons, thus to strengthen the norm against their acquisition and use.

It is hard to square the Carnegie Endowment's support for the Thirteen Steps with its view that the U.S. must retain nuclear weapons "for as long as nuclear threats remain in the world." That is the precise problem: the failure of the nuclear weapons states to negotiate elimination results in retention, which then undermines non-proliferation efforts. Another prestigious research centre, the British American Security Information Council (BASIC), addressed this point:

> …While the U.S. will want to focus on issues such as the Additional Protocol and the fuel cycle, its own provocative nuclear weapons policies will significantly hamper its negotiation maneuverability and weaken the over-all non-proliferation regime.

What Washington says and does about nuclear weapons can have a profound effect on other countries. If the United States places more reliance on nuclear weapons, other nations will follow. The power of U.S. example should not be under-estimated. Regrettably, with respect to its Article VI commitments under the NPT, the United States is currently leading by the wrong example.

Public Debate Sorely Overdue

Robert McNamara's critique of U.S. nuclear policy is well corroborated. But is the U.S. government listening to his warning? If the U.S. continues its nuclear stance, he says, substantial proliferation of nuclear weapons will almost surely follow. Some, or all, of such nations as Egypt, Japan, Saudi Arabia, Syria and Taiwan will very likely initiate nuclear weapons programs, increasing both the risk of the use of the weapons and the diversion of weapons and fissile materials into the hands of terrorists. There is little doubt that terrorists could construct a primitive device if they acquired the requisite enriched uranium. McNamara quoted another former U.S. Secretary of Defense, William J. Perry: "I have never been more fearful of a nuclear detonation than now.... There is a greater than 50 per cent probability of a nuclear strike on U.S. targets within a decade." McNamara added: "I share his fears." He called for a national debate examining the military utility of nuclear weapons: the risk of inadvertent or accidental use; the moral and legal considerations; the impact of current policies on proliferation.

A public debate on nuclear weapons, sorely overdue, would see the U.S. case demolished quickly. The U.S. reductions are a cover for the continued modernization of nuclear weapons. *Quantitative* reductions plus *qualitative* improvements do not equal elimination. Bruce Blair, President of the Washington-based Center for Defense Information, says the U.S. officials he has interviewed over the years have never expressed any belief that the U.S. intends to abolish its nuclear arsenals.

A public debate would counter this position with the stand taken by the Non-Aligned Movement. At the NPT conference, it repeated the call it has made over the years:

> The negotiation of a phased programme for the complete elimination of nuclear weapons with a specified time frame, including a Nuclear Weapons Convention, is necessary and should commence without delay.

This is a clear-cut position. It is objective and reasonable. It is a timely response to the crisis of today. There is not a hint of "unilateral" disarmament about it. The disarmament that would follow such negotiations would be mutual, verifiable and assured. The architecture to maintain security in a nuclear weapons–free world would have to be built before the last nuclear weapon is destroyed. I will discuss this architecture later in the book. The year in which the world gets to zero nuclear weapons is not important at this point. What is vital is that nations start down this path together.

The 2005 NPT conference was a golden opportunity to start to move.

3

A Sunflower and an Asterisk

On the final day of the 2005 Non-Proliferation Treaty (NPT) Review Conference, the mood was sullen. Fully 15 of the 20 working days had been consumed by procedural wrangling. There was no hope of any substantive agreement. To brighten up the atmosphere, representatives of the few remaining non-governmental organizations (NGOs) spent some of their meagre funds to buy about a hundred sunflowers to hand out to the delegates on their way into the closing plenary as a symbol of peace. It was a good idea but it ran afoul of the U.N. bureaucracy. The final session was held in the U.N. General Assembly Hall where the public is confined to the upper balcony. Security officers would not permit the NGOs access to the delegates. The diplomats sat paralyzed in their seats. The members of civil society looked down from above, feeling disappointed and rejected. The sunflowers wilted. The gap between the two worlds symbolized perfectly the deep fissures in the international community on nuclear weapons.

The sunflower was one symbol of the NPT deadlock. Another was that typographical character the asterisk. It seems absurd that the urgent calls of Kofi Annan and Mohamed ElBaradei should be reduced to an *, but that is what happened. After days of diplomatic jousting over the agenda – virtually every state wanted a reference to the 1995 and 2000 commitments, but the U.S., aided at times by France, refused – the president of the conference, Ambassador Sergio Duarte of Brazil, inserted an ★ after the words "Review of the Operation of the Treaty." To find out what the ★ referred to, one had to search out another document, which was a statement by the president. "It is understood that the review will be conducted in the light of the decision and the resolution of previous conferences, and allow discussion of any issue raised by States Parties." This compromise saved the Conference from total collapse. But to have the future of humanity trivialized by an ★ is an insult to everyone's intelligence.

The contrast between the inaction of the delegates and the hopes expressed by the NGOs, articulated in 15 speeches made to the delegates one afternoon in one of the committee rooms, was startling. Natalie Wasley and Tina Keim spoke for a group of young people from several nations:

> We ask you: What do you intend to turn over to us, the next generation? Will you give us a world in which disarmament exists on paper while billions are spent to develop the ultimate in war technology and the means of mass murder? Will you give us nations that, while deploying and developing their own nuclear weapons, are quick to go to war when enemies appear to be obtaining similar weapons? Or will you give us a world united under a common constitution that limits military armaments and eliminates entirely the possibility of nuclear holocaust? Will you be able to explain your choice in good conscience to your children and grandchildren?

Felix Fellmer of the International Law Campaign made an appeal to the delegates on behalf of all the NGO representatives. The goal of abolishing nuclear weapons may seem unrealistic now, he said, but it is equally unrealistic to believe that the world can go on as it has for any length of time without the NPT collapsing. "It is vital that you save it by making mature decisions about the future of this world and courageously stepping forward to meet this challenge."

The challenge, however, cannot be met by diplomats at the operational level. As the NPT conference showed, nuclear disarmament discussions are operating at too low a level in politics and diplomacy. Not a single national leader showed up for the conference; only Russian President Vladimir Putin sent a personal message. This led Kofi Annan, at the conclusion of the conference, to call on heads of governments to show some leadership to break the deadlock on the pressing challenges of nuclear non-proliferation and disarmament. "If they fail to do so, their peoples will ask how, in today's world, they could not find common ground in the cause of diminishing the existential threat of nuclear weapons."

In the end, the NPT conference merely reflected, rather than mended, the deep rifts over nuclear weapons.

Nuclear Energy: the NPT's Loophole

While nuclear disarmament is one such rift, another is control over the use of nuclear fuels. Iran and North Korea, by their actions, have shown the loophole in the NPT. They have been charged with using or seeking to use the benefits of the NPT to acquire nuclear technologies and fuels allegedly for peaceful purposes and then clandestinely enriching uranium for a nuclear weapon. North Korea boasts that it has produced nuclear weapons; Iran denies doing so or diverting materials. The U.S. has led the attack on both countries and urged exporting countries to deny nuclear technology to states that did not have it before. The developing countries charge that such denial is a violation of Article IV of the NPT, which describes the "inalienable right" of all parties to research, produce and use nuclear energy for peaceful purposes. They see this as one more discriminatory action by the powerful states against the weak and claim that the original NPT bargain is being further eroded.

Yet something must be done to ensure that nuclear fuels are not diverted to weaponry. Any misuse of the NPT to acquire a nuclear weapon must be stopped. In fact, the "inalienable right" can only be exercised in conformity with Articles I and II, which proscribe the transfer or receipt of nuclear weapons. But what happens when a country acquires nuclear materials for peaceful purposes and then, having achieved the capacity to make a nuclear bomb, leaves the NPT? This is the loophole that must be closed. Any solution must protect both the goal of guaranteeing the non-proliferation of nuclear weapons and the right to develop civilian nuclear industries. In other words, the right to nuclear energy must be preserved while ensuring it does not become a route to nuclear weapons. The clandestine pursuit of nuclear weapons challenges international law.

This tension is becoming more acute as the demand for nuclear fuels grows and the developing countries clamour for full access. There is a common misperception that nuclear power plants are on their way out. On the contrary, energy ministers from many countries are convinced that only by building more nuclear power stations can the world meet its soaring energy needs while averting environmental disaster. In the past, the virtual absence of restrictions or taxes on greenhouse gas emissions from oil, coal and gas plants has meant that nuclear power's advantage, low emissions, had no tangible economic value. But the entry-into-force of the Kyoto Protocol, requiring plant operators to pay for their pollution, combined with soaring fossil fuel costs, is persuading countries to intensify nuclear production.

Moreover, when we consider the positive aspect of "atoms for peace," the growing role of nuclear energy seems assured. Nuclear science plays a key role in enabling humanitarian benefits essential to development: diagnosing and curing cancer; providing higher yielding, disease-resistant crops; reducing airborne and waterborne pollution; and, not least, producing 16 per cent of the world's electricity with almost no greenhouse gas emissions.

However, nuclear power is highly controversial because, while the nuclear reactor does not directly produce any greenhouse gases, the nuclear fuel chain, and especially the production of the materials needed to build nuclear power plants, is a significant source of such emissions. And any accident, as the Chernobyl and Three Mile Island tragedies showed, can release radiation contaminating large areas. Further, the disposal of radioactive waste remains a vexing problem in all the nuclear countries. Opponents of nuclear energy want governments to put much more funding into alternative energy programs, such as for solar and wind power and other renewable resources. The debate over the efficacy of nuclear power goes on. Meanwhile, many developing countries are demanding access to nuclear technologies through the provisions of the NPT.

The U.N.'s High-Level Panel on Threats, Challenges and Change addressed this problem and said two remedies are required. First, the International Atomic Energy Agency's (IAEA) inspection and verification rules must be tightened up by making the Additional Protocol the universal standard for IAEA safeguards. The Additional Protocol was adopted in 1997 to give the IAEA more inspection rights, but only one third of states have ratified it. Also, the U.N. Security Council must be prepared to act in cases of non-compliance. Second, negotiations should be started to make the IAEA a guarantor for the supply of fissile material to civilian power users; thus, the IAEA would guarantee the uninterrupted supply of nuclear services at market rates. To get this process started, states should surrender their right to construct such facilities and voluntarily institute a moratorium on the construction of enrichment or reprocessing facilities. Further, the panel said that any state withdrawing from the NPT (as North Korea has done) should be held responsible for violations committed while still a party to it. The Security Council should examine any withdrawal.

Before the 2005 Review Conference began, Mohamed ElBaradei tried to show a way out of the dilemma. Institute a five-year moratorium on new facilities for uranium enrichment and plutonium separation, he said, and guarantee an economical supply of nuclear fuel to bona fide users. Then convert all reactors using highly enriched uranium to low uranium (which cannot be used for bombs).

But the participants in the Review Conference could not muster support for any decisive action to close the loophole. The draft report of the committee studying this issue merely called for stronger support for existing IAEA safeguards and the suspension of nuclear co-operation with states in violation of their non-proliferation and safeguards obligations. Unfortunately, even this report, weak as it was, went down in the crossfire over issues related to the Middle East.

The Divisive Middle East

The Middle East figured prominently in the package deal arrived at in 1995 when the NPT was indefinitely extended. The Arab states, led by Egypt, protested strongly that, while they were subscribing to the tenets of the NPT, their neighbour Israel possessed nuclear weapons, had unsafeguarded nuclear facilities and even refused to join the NPT – all with Western complicity. It is believed that Israel possesses about 200 nuclear weapons, although it refuses to confirm or deny this.

To get Arab support for the NPT extension, the 1995 conference adopted a resolution calling on all states in the Middle East – without exception – to accede to the NPT and place their nuclear facilities under full-scope IAEA safeguards. Israel has continued to ignore this global call and thus the establishment of a nuclear weapons–free zone in the

Middle East appears farther off than ever. Israel argues that a comprehensive peace settlement in the Middle East is a precondition to any move on the nuclear front. Arab states claim that Israel is getting nuclear help from the West despite the strictures of the NPT. Again, Egypt is leading the fight to put more pressure on Israel, demanding tougher rules to exclude the transfer of nuclear-related material to Israel and to deny Israeli scientists and researchers access to U.S. nuclear laboratories. Egypt also wanted a standing committee to deal directly with Israel to bring it into the NPT.

When Egypt argued its case at the Review Conference, Western states replied with more ambiguity and refused to implement the 1995 resolution. Since the resolution was an integral part of the NPT extension, Egypt argued that the NPT as a whole is compromised. Then, to add insult to injury, Egypt was particularly incensed at the idea that it and other developing countries should be subject to even more stringent rules attached to the nuclear fuel cycle while the U.S. and the rest of the West stand mutely by as Israel continues to ignore the call to join the NPT and put its nuclear facilities under IAEA safeguards.

Throughout the month, Egypt fought for the integrity of the NPT, adopting obstreperous tactics. But in so doing, it alienated many countries, particularly its partners in the New Agenda Coalition. This is a group of seven countries (Brazil, Egypt, Ireland, Mexico, New Zealand, South Africa and Sweden) formed in 1998 to press the nuclear weapons states to fulfill their commitments to nuclear disarmament. The New Agenda Coalition has always used moderate tactics to gain more support and, in 2004, was supported by eight NATO states. This showed the possibility of building a strong centre of moderate, non-nuclear states to develop leverage against the nuclear weapons states. But the U.S. and its Western nuclear partners have rejected even appeals for moderate gains in nuclear disarmament.

The growing strains between those in the New Agenda Coalition who want to take a more aggressive stance and those such as Ireland and Sweden, who feel a moderate agenda is more attainable, have started to become very pronounced. Then, when Egypt, frequently supported by South Africa, vociferously objected to tightening the rules on the nuclear fuel cycle because Israel is getting off scot-free on these issues, the New Agenda Coalition bond suffered a severe blow. The group's usual internal coordination on nuclear disarmament was severely challenged when proliferation concerns moved to centre stage. It was an irony of the conference that it was Egypt that frequently denied consensus when it was actually the U.S. that undermined the integrity of the NPT by focusing almost exclusively on non-proliferation to the detriment of disarmament obligations.

NATO: Trapped in Contradiction

The nuclear fuel cycle is not the only loophole in the NPT that needs to be closed. Articles I and II explicitly forbid transferring and receiving nuclear weapons between a nuclear weapons state and a non-nuclear weapons state. Nonetheless, for many years, the U.S. has stationed nuclear weapons in Europe. A recent report by the Natural Resources Defense Council says the U.S. maintains 480 tactical nuclear weapons in five non-nuclear NATO states, Belgium, Germany, Italy, the Netherlands and Turkey as well as its fellow nuclear weapons state, the United Kingdom. NATO has always insisted that sharing weapons is compatible with the NPT because the U.S. maintains control over the weapons until a time of war, at which point the NPT would no longer be in effect. However, it has never been established that the NPT is only legal in peacetime. In any event, NATO asserts that its sharing of nuclear weapons (as with the existence of nuclear weapons) predates the NPT.

NATO's core policy is that nuclear weapons are "essential" and provide the "supreme guarantee" of security. On June 9, 2005, a few days after the NPT Review Conference ended, NATO reaffirmed the "continued validity" of its nuclear policy and stated, "The nuclear forces based in Europe and committed to NATO continue to provide an essential political and military link between the European and North American members of the Alliance." To justify its nuclear weapons through an appeal to solidarity of its members shows the bankruptcy of NATO policy. On what rational grounds can it be argued that nuclear weapons constitute a binding element? The policy shows a contempt for the international law that the NPT represents.

All NATO states signed on to the "unequivocal undertaking" to eliminate nuclear weapons through the Thirteen Steps (see Chapter 2); yet they give their loyalty to a military alliance that says nuclear weapons are the "supreme guarantee" of their security. The contradiction is blatant and it prevents the middle-power members of NATO from playing a more effective role in pushing for nuclear disarmament. They are trapped in their own alliance, dominated by the U.S., the U.K. and France, the three nuclear NATO states.

NATO asserts that it has cut the number of tactical nuclear weapons in Europe, but continues to need them, it says, "to preserve peace and prevent coercion." The doublespeak is breathtaking. NATO seems not to care that its insistence on maintaining nuclear weapons sends the wrong message to militaries, governments and the public around the world, namely that the possession of nuclear weapons is legitimate, necessary for true security and the defining characteristic of powerful states. The alliance seem oblivious to its own hypocrisy as it opposes the possession of nuclear weapons by any other state while reserving to itself the right to deploy them.

Of course, the problem of tactical nuclear weapons in Europe is not just NATO's. Russia also possesses them, and it reported to the Review Conference that it has reduced the number of tactical nuclear weapons inherited from the Soviet Union by three quarters. It refuses to say how many it has, but the number is certainly in the thousands. Some estimates put the total of U.S. and Russian tactical weapons at 7,000 at least. However, Russia draws a distinction between its possession and that of the U.S.: whereas Russia confines them to its own territory, the U.S. has them in five ostensibly non-nuclear countries as well as the U.K. Russia wants the U.S. to pull its tactical nuclear weapons out of Europe as a condition of negotiating the complete elimination of tactical weapons.

American allies are silent on this subject. NATO planners know that the rationale for the NATO doctrine would disappear if tactical nuclear weapons are removed from Europe. And if NATO were to take a new position that nuclear weapons are not, after all, essential, would that not undermine U.S. military doctrine? Despite the bad example it is giving the rest of the world, NATO remains obdurate.

Why then would Russia not be concerned? NATO is an expanding alliance. The 12 countries that founded NATO in 1949 have grown to 26, with a combined population of 880 million. Nearly one in six people on earth now live under the nuclear umbrella of the Western military alliance. NATO says it has no intention of stationing nuclear weapons in the territory of its new members. That is no answer. When the number of countries committed to supporting and planning for the use of nuclear weapons is actually increasing, the NPT cannot be fulfilled.

However, there are signs of movement. In 2005, the Belgian Senate passed a resolution calling for the removal of U.S. tactical nuclear weapons from Belgium. And the European Union took a step forward in calling for negotiations on "an effectively verifiable agreement to best achieve the greatest reduction of these weapons." Main Committee I of the NPT Review Conference addressed this issue, and the chairman's draft report included a passage that called upon the nuclear weapons states "to refrain from nuclear sharing for military purposes under any kind of security arrangements, among themselves, with non-nuclear weapons states and with states not party to the Treaty." The U.S. vigorously objected.

The NPT Review Conference failed to fully articulate, let alone resolve, this issue. But one way or another, NATO's nuclear policies are coming under renewed attention and NATO may have to respond if the Europeans take up the issue.

The restlessness of NATO countries with the overbearing attitude of their three nuclear colleagues was further revealed in a paper on preserving the integrity of the NPT submitted by seven NATO states led by the Netherlands (the others were Belgium, Lithuania, Norway, Spain, Poland and Turkey). The paper gave strong backing to the 2000 Review Conference commitments, pointed to the need for irreversibility and transparency in the Moscow Treaty, urged a diminished role for nuclear weapons in security policies, and supported the extension of nuclear weapons–free zones. It gave strong support for legally binding security assurances, full ratification of the Comprehensive Test Ban Treaty and "reduction and ultimate elimination" of tactical nuclear weapons. U.S. officials made it known informally that the U.S. was not pleased with this softening of support within NATO for nuclear weapons.

Expanding Nuclear Weapons–Free Zones

The growth of nuclear weapons–free zones is becoming an important part of the nuclear debate. It is often overlooked that virtually the entire southern hemisphere is free of nuclear weapons. This is because many states have banded together through regional treaties to ban nuclear weapons from their areas. The 1967 Treaty of Tlatelolco, which banned nuclear weapons in Latin America and the Caribbean, set the standard for subsequent treaties, and three more have been created since 1967:

- the 1985 Treaty of Rarotonga, covering the South Pacific;
- the 1996 Treaty of Bangkok, covering Southeast Asia; and
- the 1997 Treaty of Pelindaba, covering Africa.

The continent of Antarctica is nuclear-free under the provisions of the 1959 Antarctic Treaty. So are the Earth's orbit and all celestial bodies under the 1967 Outer Space Treaty.

In 2000, led by Brazil and New Zealand, the U.N. General Assembly called for the unification of the current nuclear weapons–free zones under a southern hemisphere treaty. As a step towards this goal, Mexico hosted the International Conference of countries that are currently parties to nuclear weapons–free zone treaties in April 2005, on the eve of the NPT Review Conference. Representatives of 110 countries attended and unanimously adopted a strong declaration calling for more zones as an effective means for achieving total elimination of nuclear weapons. The declaration said in part:

> We reaffirm that the continued existence of nuclear weapons constitutes a threat to all humanity and that their use would have catastrophic consequences for life on Earth. Therefore, we believe in the need to move toward the priority objective of nuclear disarmament and to achieve the total elimination and prohibition of nuclear weapons....
>
> We reaffirm that the use or threat of use of nuclear weapons constitutes a breach of international law and the United Nations Charter, and a crime against humanity.

The declaration called for establishing nuclear weapons—free zones in the Middle East, South Asia, Northeast Asia and Central Europe. These proposed nuclear weapons—free zones differ significantly from previous ones, in that they all include or border on de facto or declared nuclear weapons states. As the British American Security Information Council noted, "They also indicate a transition from a passive but legally protected region to a region where disarmament is carried out." Establishing a central European zone, for example, would require the actual withdrawal, dismantling and destruction of nuclear weapons.

The Mexico conference showed not only that nuclear weapons—free zones are a way to a nuclear weapons—free world, but also that significant gains can be made when like-minded nations work together. It was a lesson, unfortunately, lost on participants at the NPT Review Conference.

The subject of nuclear weapons—free zones is closely connected to the issue of security assurances, which have long been a contentious issue at NPT conferences. A security assurance is any type of assistance a state receives from or is promised by an outside source that contributes to its security. Assurances fall into two broad categories. Positive assurances are those that contribute to a state's ability to defend itself against attack. Negative assurances are promises not to attack a state.

It is commonly held that positive assurances, such as nuclear umbrellas under alliances, and negative assurances, such as no-first-use pledges, have contributed significantly to non-proliferation. South Korea's and Japan's interest in nuclear weapons declined rapidly after the U.S. strengthened its security commitments to those states. Members of NATO and the defunct Warsaw Pact were also the beneficiaries of nuclear umbrellas provided by the U.S. and the former Soviet Union.

On the other hand, India, Pakistan, Israel and South Africa all sought alliance relationships with nuclear weapons states and, after failing to achieve them, proceeded to develop their own undeclared nuclear weapons capability (South Africa gave up its nuclear weapons in 1991). In the case of India, failure to obtain security assurances led to its persistent criticism of the NPT. India argued that in exchange for its promise to remain non-nuclear, the nuclear weapons states either had to be prepared to defend the non-nuclear weapons states from nuclear attack, or had to agree not to use nuclear weapons against them. Without this, the NPT bargain was incomplete. Responding, the U.N. Security Council adopted, in 1968, Resolution 255, which promised assistance to any non-nuclear weapons state party to the NPT that was a victim of nuclear aggression. India (and many non-nuclear weapons states) regarded this assurance as too weak.

On the eve of the 1995 NPT Review and Extension Conference, the nuclear weapons states embodied a new set of assurances in Security Council Resolution 984, which articulates more clearly than ever specific actions to be taken by the Security Council in the event of a nuclear weapons threat against a non-nuclear weapons state. A state may request "urgent action" by the Security Council; investigation of disputes; technical, medical or humanitarian assistance; and compensation from the aggressor for loss. The NWS considered their efforts to update assurances a great step forward.

However, since Resolution 984 is not legally binding, many non-nuclear weapons states proclaimed their right to receive "unconditional, universal and legally binding" security assurances. They also protested the continuing refusal of four nuclear weapons states to give a no-first-use pledge (only China had done so).

The best the 2000 NPT conference could do was to declare, "The total elimination of nuclear weapons is the only absolute guarantee against the use or threat of use of nuclear weapons." It put the issue of obtaining legally binding security assurances over to 2005. The subsequent move by the Bush administration to threaten aggressors who used chemical or biological weapons with the use of nuclear weapons raised the heat on this issue, especially with the U.S. in the process of developing its "bunker-buster."

The Non-Aligned Movement came into the 2005 conference with a renewed demand for "a universal, unconditional and legally binding instrument on security assurances." Again, the nuclear weapons states balked and tightened the screws on the non-nuclear states by insisting that the assurances that do exist (although not legally binding) would not be applicable if any state were in material breach of its own non-proliferation and disarmament obligations. The reference to Iran was unmistakable.

The nuclear weapons states did offer to provide future security assurances to states living in nuclear weapons–free zones. This is a hollow promise as far as Europe is concerned, since NATO's nuclear policies prevent a nuclear weapons–free zone from being created in Central Europe. What all this amounts to is that the nuclear weapons states are keeping their legal options open for the use of nuclear weapons, while proscribing the acquisition of nuclear weapons by any other state.

A Troubling Equation

5 nuclear weapons states + 3 unrecognized nuclear weapon states – 1 withdrawn state, multiplied by x number of non-state actors seeking nuclear weapons, divided by 60 years since the Hiroshima and Nagasaki bombings, multiplied by 1,732 NGO representatives at the Review Conference. Put that in parentheses and divide it by the number of days left at this Review Conference and multiply it by the 35 years that have passed since the nuclear weapon states first undertook to "pursue negotiations in good faith on effective measures relating to cessation of the nuclear arms race at an early date and to nuclear disarmament." Add that to the number of hours spent negotiating these procedural issues and tell us: are we any closer to a nuclear weapon-free world?

News in Review, *May 13, 2005 (daily report published at the 2005 Review Conference by Reaching Critical Will)*

"A Treaty Worth Fighting For"

The 2005 Review Conference stumbled to the end, having spent $3 million in the process. U.N. Under-Secretary-General Nobuyasu Abe presented this figure as "three Cadillacs per day" (3 x $50,000 x 20). The U.S. paid 32.8 per cent of the costs. Iran paid 0.115 per cent. Is it any wonder the U.S. dominates U.N. proceedings when it pays such a hefty amount of the bill?

The only matter of substance to make it through the procedural hurdles was the report of Main Committee I, on nuclear disarmament and assurances, although even here it was stated that there was "no consensus." Nevertheless, it was evident that many, if not most states, did support its principal findings.

- Nuclear weapons states must stop sharing nuclear weapons for military purposes under any kind of security arrangement.

- The most effective way to prevent nuclear terrorism is the total elimination of nuclear weapons.

- International action to stop proliferation is essential.

- Building upon the decisions taken at the 1995 and 2000 Review Conferences, including the "unequivocal undertaking" for total nuclear disarmament, no new nuclear weapons should be developed.

- Anticipating the early entry-into-force of the Comprehensive Test Ban Treaty (CTBT), the moratorium on testing should be maintained.

- The nuclear weapons states must respect existing commitments regarding security assurances, pending the conclusion of multilaterally negotiated legally binding security assurances for NPT parties.

With this material to work on, the conference was far from pointless. Key issues have been identified. The international community cannot stop moving forward just because of the intransigence of the nuclear weapons states. The mood, however, was bleak.

Delegates seemed too embarrassed even to discuss the committee reports at the open plenary session that closed the conference. Twenty-four delegations made closing speeches, with lamentation the common theme: Japan: "extremely regrettable"; Brazil: "deep sense of frustration"; Norway: "profoundly disappointed"; Cuba: "sincerely regret"; Ukraine: "unfortunate"; Chile: "frustration and displeasure."

The two protagonists, the U.S. and Iran, devoted their closing comments to attacking each other once again. The U.S. said, "Iran's single-minded pursuit of uranium enrichment capability, which we firmly believe is intended to underpin a nuclear weapons program, raises a key question": unnecessary proliferation of such facilities adds to the danger of weapons proliferation. That is why President Bush proposed closing the NPT loophole to stop a state from pursuing enrichment and reprocessing equipment for ostensibly peaceful purposes while planning all along to use that capacity to manufacture material for nuclear weapons.

Iran, which, as it turned out, had the last word at the conference, criticized the U.S. for developing new nuclear weapons systems, maintaining tactical nuclear weapons in Europe, abrogating the Anti-Ballistic Missile Treaty, rejecting the CTBT, threatening non-nuclear weapons states, aiding Israeli nuclear scientists and wanting the conference to fail so that it could pursue programs to restrict access to nuclear fuels and technologies in other forums it dominates.

The most thoughtful and effective closing comment was made by Ambassador Paul Meyer of Canada. "We have let the pursuit of short-term, parochial interests override the collective long-term interest in sustaining this Treaty's authority and integrity," he said.

We have witnessed intransigence from more than one State on pressing issues of the day, coupled with the hubris that demands the priorities of the many be subordinated to the preferences of the few....

If there is a silver lining in the otherwise dark cloud of this Review Conference, it lies in the hope that our leaders and citizens will be so concerned by its failure that they mobilize behind prompt remedial action....

This is a treaty worth fighting for and we are not prepared to stand idly by while its crucial supports are undermined.

Look at this last sentence again: "This is a treaty worth fighting for and we are not prepared to stand idly by while its crucial supports are undermined." This is an interesting position, coming from a neighbour of the United States, which today stands as the biggest obstacle to nuclear disarmament. Are there other like-minded states that feel as betrayed as Canada does? Will they start speaking up? Where will the new jolt of energy come from to overcome the debacle of the 2005 NPT Review Conference?

PART II

The Dangers Are Multiplying

4

The Message of the Hibakusha

The survivors of the atomic bombings of Hiroshima and Nagasaki are known as *hibakusha*. One of the Hiroshima *hibakusha*, a young woman who was a few blocks from the centre of the blast on August 6, 1945, told her story:

> Somewhere a voice shouted, "Hey, there's a parachute. A parachute is coming down!" Without thinking, I looked in the direction indicated by the voice. At that instant, flash. The sky in the direction I was looking was pure light. I don't know how to describe that light like a fire burning in my eyes. It was like the eerie bluish-purple sparks that electric street cars make at night, only trillions of times brighter. But that isn't exactly right either. So fast that later I wondered which came first, the light was followed by a roar that reverberated to the bottom of my belly, and I was instantly slammed hard against the ground, with something falling in little pieces on my head and shoulders. When I opened my eyes, I saw nothing but darkness.

> Suddenly I clearly saw the faces of my three children, who had been evacuated to the country. Thinking of them made me begin impulsively, involuntarily thrashing my body around violently. I pushed and

pushed with my hands to sweep away the pieces of wood and tile, but more kept sliding in on me, and I couldn't seem to get my body free. "I can't die. What will the children do? My husband might be dead. I have to get out of here." In utter desperation I crawled out.

Once out, I noticed a terrible stench in the air. "It must have been a white phosphorous fire bomb." Without thinking, I took the towel that was tucked into my belt and firmly wiped my nose and mouth. That was when I realized for the first time that there was something wrong with my face. The skin that I wiped just peeled and slipped right off. I was shocked.

"What? My arm!" The skin on my right hand slipped off from the second joint of my fingers and just dangled sickeningly from the tips of my fingers. The fingers on my left hand, from the wrist down, were peeled raw and slimy.

The woman fled in a dream-like state and made it to a relief station in the suburbs. Summer turned to autumn and still her flesh continued to melt away. Her wounds were the colour of a crushed, ripe tomato, but no new skin would form. The following spring, her bandages finally came off. She described her physical condition:

My left earlobe had shrunk to half its size. On my left cheek, down past my mouth and onto my neck was a keloid the size of a person's palm. On my right hand, a five-centimeter-wide keloid ran from the second joint to my little finger. The five fingers of my left hand had pulled together abnormally where they joined the hand.

In 1995, Takashi Hiraoka, then the mayor of Hiroshima, told this story during the International Court of Justice hearings on the legality of nuclear weapons to illustrate the horror of the Hiroshima bombing. "I am here," he told the Court, "to represent the hundreds of thousands of victims whose lives were cut short and survivors who are still suffering the effects of radiation fifty years later."

The bomb used a small amount of uranium 235 to produce energy equivalent to 15 kilotons of TNT. A B-29, the world's largest bomber in 1945, carried a maximum payload of five tons of TNT in conventional weapons. Thus, the atomic bomb was equivalent to the instantaneous attack of more than 3,000 B-29s.

An intense flash of light flooded the city centre. With the roar of the blast that followed, enormous pillars of flame burst towards the skies. Most buildings crumbled. A wind of nearly 1,000 miles an hour tore through the city. Hospitals were in ruins, medical staff were dead or injured and there was no medicine or equipment. Despite their own burns and injuries, survivors worked frantically to help others, but after a few days or weeks, fever, diarrhea, hemorrhaging and extreme fatigue claimed many more lives. Within five months, 140,000 people, more than one third of the population of Hiroshima, were dead.

Three days after the Hiroshima attack, Nagasaki was decimated by the second atomic bomb. Nagasaki mayor Iccoh Itoh brought the story of his city's devastation to the International Court of Justice. The city of Kokura was the original target of the second attack, but because of poor visibility the American bomber flew to a secondary target, Nagasaki. When the bombardier caught a glimpse of the city through a crack in the clouds, he hastily released the bomb. The centre of Nagasaki was supposed to be the target, but the bomb struck the Urakami district, home to a large Christian population that had kept the light of faith alive during a long period of persecution from the seventeenth through the nineteenth centuries. The bomb laid the neighbourhood to waste and instantly killed 8,500 of the 12,000

Christians living there. Mayor Itoh's graphic description of what happened has been quoted many times:

> The explosion of the atomic bomb generated an enormous fireball, 200 meters in radius, almost as though a small sun had appeared in the sky. The next instant, a ferocious blast and wave of heat assailed the ground with a thunderous roar. The surface temperature of the fireball was about 7000 degrees C, and the heat rays that reached the ground were over 3000 degrees C. The explosion instantly killed or injured people within a two-kilometer radius of the hypocenter, leaving innumerable corpses charred like clumps of charcoal and scattered in the ruins near the hypocenter. In some cases not even a trace of the person's remains could be found. The blast wind of over 300 meters per second slapped down trees and demolished most buildings. Even iron-reinforced concrete structures were so badly damaged that they seemed to have been smashed by a giant hammer. The fierce flash of heat meanwhile melted glass and left metal objects contorted like strands of taffy, and the subsequent fires burned the ruins of the city to ashes.

Nagasaki became a city of death where not even the sounds of insects could be heard. After a while, countless men, women and children began to gather for a drink of water at the banks of nearby Urakami River, their hair and clothing scorched and their burnt skin hanging off in sheets like rags. Begging for help they died one after another in the water or in heaps on the banks. Then radiation began to take its toll, killing people like a scourge of death expanding in concentric circles from the hypocenter. Four months after the atomic bombing, 74,000 people were dead and 75,000 had suffered injuries, that is, two thirds of the city population had fallen victim to this calamity that came upon Nagasaki like a preview of the Apocalypse.

Holding up a large photo, he told the Court:

Now please look at this photo…taken on the day after the Nagasaki atomic bombing. The boy seems to be enjoying an afternoon nap on the sunlit veranda of his house. The boy, however, is dead. He had died instantly in the ferocious blast, probably not even noticing that a bomb had exploded or that he was falling into an eternal sleep….This photo shows the carbonized corpse of a boy perhaps four years old who was exposed to the bombing near the hypocenter. What crime did these children commit? Did they take up guns and point them at the enemy?… All the leaders of the nuclear States should come to Nagasaki to see this photograph. They should take a direct look at the reality of nuclear weapons and realize the nature of what happened in front of the eyes of these children that day. Let the leaders hear the silent screams of these children.

When I first visited Hiroshima and Nagasaki, I too felt that every political leader – everyone even remotely connected to decision-making processes about the maintenance of nuclear weapons – should be forced to journey to both cities and interview the *hibakusha*, tour the museums and touch the relics. Then the reality of the words of Robert Oppenheimer, one of the fathers of the bomb who later turned against it, would hit home: "I have become death, the shatterer of worlds."

Not everyone, of course, can travel to Japan to have this experience. But the vivid testimony of the *hibakusha* is but a click away at the "Voice of Hibakusha" website (www.inicom.com/hibakusha/).

• Akira Onogi, 16 years old at the time, was 1.2 km from the centre of the explosion:

What impressed me very strongly was a 5 or 6 year-old-boy with his right leg cut at the thigh. He was hopping on his left foot to cross over the bridge. I can still record this scene very clearly. The water of the river now is very clean and clear, but on the day of bombing, all the houses along this river were blown by the blast with their pillars, beams and pieces of furniture blown into the river or hanging off the bridges. The river was also filled with dead people blown by the blast and with survivors who came here to seek water. Anyway, I could not see the surface of the water at all. Many injured people with peeled skin were crying out for help. Obviously, they were looking at us and we could hardly turn our eyes toward the river.

• Yosaku Mikami, a fireman, was 1.9 km from the centre:

Since our order was to help the most heavily injured, we searched for them. We tried to open the eyes of the injured and we found out they were still alive. We tried to carry them by their arms and legs and to place them onto the fire truck. But this was difficult because their skin was peeled off as we tried to move them. They were all heavily burned. They never complained, but they felt pain even when their skin was peeling off. We carried the victims to the prefecture hospital.

• Hiroshi Sawachika was an army doctor four kilometres away:

We doctors learned a lot...through the suffering of all those people.... I learned that nuclear weapons which gnaw the minds and bodies of human beings should never be used. Even the slightest idea of using nuclear arms should be completely exterminated from the minds of human beings. Otherwise, we will repeat the same tragedy. And we will never stop being ashamed of ourselves.

• Toshiko Saeki was 26 at the time of the bombing. She was at her parents' home in Yasufuruichi with her children. Returning to Hiroshima on the afternoon of August 6, she searched for her other relatives for many days, but was not able to find them. Ms. Saeki lost thirteen members of her family in the A-bomb attack.

By the end of August, maybe around, oh, the 28th or so, my hair started to fall out, I vomited blood. My teeth were coming out. And I have a fever of about 40 degrees. Nuclear war has nothing good. Whether you win or lose, it leaves you feeling futile with only your rage and with fear about the after-effects of radioactivity. The survivors have to live with this fear. At times I have thought I should have died then, it would have been better. But I must live for the sake of the people, all the people who lost their lives. So I relate my experience hoping that my talk would discourage people from making war. Our experience must not be forgotten. What we believed in during the war turned out to be worth nothing. We don't know to whom we should turn our rage. I went through hell on earth. Hiroshima should not be repeated again. That is why I keep telling the same old story over and over again. And I'll keep repeating it.

Psychic Numbing

Unfortunately, the catastrophic experiences of Hiroshima and Nagasaki are fading from the public mind. I noticed a trend in the thinking of the students I taught at the University of Alberta: for them Hiroshima and Nagasaki were historical abstractions, events that occurred long ago without much meaning for the post–Cold War age. When I went on speaking tours across Canada to discuss modern nuclear policy with concerned citizens, I would often be asked why I was concentrating on nuclear weapons, which had not killed anyone for more than half a century, and neglecting to emphasize land mines, which are killing and maiming children today. The public has seen many photos of children maimed by land mines and were understandably upset, but since there are no modern photos of nuclear carnage, the subject tends to be pushed aside.

One reason for this nuclear isolation is that the subject is just too big and seemingly remote to fit into everyday thinking. Another is a societal denial of such mammoth carnage or, as the psychiatrist Robert Lipton calls it, a "psychic numbing." Undeniably, governments – starting certainly with the United States government, but including that of virtually every Western country – have deliberately downplayed the effects of the very policies they uphold and shamelessly lied to their electorate that such policies were in national security interests. While polls show that the public generally feels that nuclear weapons should be done away with, there is also a schizophrenic support for security policy that has nuclear weapons at its centre. In the main, there is not much public debate about maintaining nuclear weapons policy because – even though it is horrible and focused on massive death – it is veiled in the sanctity of national security.

It is important that the stories of the *hibakusha* not be lost on coming generations. They continue to teach us. In the words of Hiroshima mayor Akiba: "We simply cannot allow something like this to happen again, period. This is the reality of a nuclear war." The first lesson of the *hibakusha* is an affirmation of life. Under conditions in which no one could have blamed them for choosing death, they chose to live. Second, they reached out to the world to listen. Third, they rejected the path of retaliation and chose instead the path of reconciliation. The *hibakusha* do not see the world as a collection of enemies.

They do not direct their feelings against the United States, the perpetrator of the suffering, but against the suffering itself. They teach us that it is futile to address the subject of Hiroshima and Nagasaki by blaming the U.S. Historians are themselves divided on whether the bomb should have been used to bring World War II to a close. Some say Japan, reeling from conventional attacks, was ready to surrender; other say not and that the atomic bombing saved American lives and perhaps more Japanese than would have been lost in a U.S. invasion of Japan. But this is beside the point. Concentrating on the U.S. political and military decision of the time diverts attention from the real task at hand: producing a consensus of all political parties in all countries to do away with nuclear weapons in the name of humanity. As awesome and terrible as the destruction of Hiroshima and Nagasaki was, it is miniscule compared to the destruction that could be wrought by today's nuclear weapons.

We need to develop a much deeper understanding in the public mind of the evil nature of nuclear weapons and move forward with political action. The International Court of Justice ruled that the heat, energy and radiation characteristic of nuclear explosions render them catastrophic. The destructive power of nuclear weapons cannot be contained in space or time. They make no distinction between combatants and non-combatants or between military installations and civilian communities: old and young, male and female, soldier and civilian – the killing is utterly indiscriminate. Nuclear weapons have the potential to destroy all civilization and the entire ecosystem of the planet. That is the message of the *hibakusha*.

Radiation is the most telling effect of the nuclear bomb. Immediately after the explosion in Hiroshima, the area was bathed in high levels of initial radiation – gamma rays and neutrons. Within a radius of one kilometre of the centre, nearly everyone who suffered full body exposure to radiation died. Those who initially managed to survive soon succumbed to the radiation's after-effects.

It is not enough to express this evil in just an abstract way. Here is the grim reality as seen by an eyewitness:

> It was a horrible sight. Hundreds of people were trying to escape to the hills past our house. The sight of them was almost unbearable. Their faces and hands were burnt and swollen and great sheets of skin had peeled away from their tissues to hang down like rags on a scarecrow. They moved like a line of ants all through the night. They passed our house but the next morning the line had stopped. I found them lying on both sides of the road so thick that it was impossible to pass without stepping on them.
>
> And they had no faces, their eyes, noses and mouths had been burnt away and it looked like their ears had been melted off. It was hard to tell front from back.

5

True MAD-ness

While the *hibakusha* went on suffering, the world's shock at the destructive power of the atom bomb quickly dissipated. For both governments and the public, there were too many other things to think about: post-war reconstruction, forming the United Nations, revving up the engine of world commerce and, later, the deepening antipathy between the United States and the Soviet Union in the Cold War. The first U.N. resolution in 1946 established the U.N. Atomic Energy Commission "to deal with the problems raised by the discovery of nuclear energy." The U.S. then proposed the Baruch Plan, named after U.S. diplomat Bernard Baruch, in which the U.S. would give up its nuclear weapons program after all states had ceded their nuclear materials to international control. The Soviet Union opposed the plan and wanted the U.S. to turn over its nuclear weapons before other countries gave up their nuclear materials. These differences could not be resolved. The Soviet Union tested its first nuclear weapon in 1949. The nuclear arms race was underway.

New technologies allowed countries to develop ever more powerful nuclear weapons and shortened the time interval from launch to impact to only minutes. The destructive power of nuclear weapons, which dwarfs that of even the most powerful conventional weapons, was gradually lost on decision makers: what counted was the race.

One side or the other was always marginally ahead in testing and deployment, so the other side caught up. The lead in the race for improved systems switched back and forth between the superpowers. The U.S. led with the atom bomb, intercontinental bomber and thermonuclear bomb. The Soviet Union caught up and plunged ahead with the intercontinental ballistic missile (ICBM) and man-made satellite. The U.S. again took the lead with the submarine-launched ballistic missile and multiple warhead. The Soviet Union countered with the anti-ballistic missile and caught up to the U.S. advance in multiple, independently targeted re-entry vehicles (MIRV). The U.S. went ahead again with the long-range cruise missile and neutron bomb. Between 1982 and 1988, the U.S. and the Soviet Union increased the number of nuclear weapons in their arsenals by more than one third – the U.S. reaching a total of 23,490; the Soviets, 40,723. Both sides continued to develop new systems of mobile launchers. Nuclear weapons testing went on regularly, at first in the atmosphere and then, after the Partial Test Ban Treaty was signed in 1963, underground. Altogether, the nuclear powers have tested nuclear weapons more than 2,000 times. It has been estimated that global fallout from nuclear testing will lead to at least two million deaths from cancer alone, not to mention other health effects.

The military strategy that led to all of this was called Mutual Assured Destruction, the acronym of which – MAD – is an entirely accurate description of the situation. Deterrence, which is based on mutual vulnerability, became its central tenet. Deterrence is said to work when both sides have the ability to inflict unacceptable damage on the other, even after having been subjected to a nuclear attack. Crucial to this idea is the assumption that neither side has the capability to launch a first strike that could completely eliminate the other's ability to retaliate. Unable to attack with impunity, the attacker is thus deterred from initiating hostilities by the knowledge that an attack would be suicidal. Over the years, the need to improve "damage limitation" and "strengthen" deterrence became reasons for the two to justify a virtually unchecked build-up and modernization of their nuclear forces.

By the 1970s, the smallest of the strategic nuclear weapons the superpowers deployed was several times more powerful than the bomb dropped on Hiroshima, and most were ten or 20 times as powerful. In less than 30 minutes, a simple missile could deliver a destructive force equivalent to 200 Hiroshima bombs to within 90 m of a target 11,000 km away. The suffering of the *hibakusha* was lost in this new frenzy of technology.

The United Kingdom, France and China all acquired nuclear technology and started building their own bombs, which brought a stunning anomaly to light: the five permanent members of the U.N. Security Council, the very states charged with maintaining peace and security in the world, became charter members of the nuclear club, brandishing weapons that threatened to destroy humanity. This truly was MAD-ness. In 1984, then Secretary-General of the United Nations, Javier Perez de Cuellar, expressed alarm. A nuclear war could lead to the extinction of humanity, he warned, and then pointed to the two superpowers: "By what right do they decide the fate of all humanity?... There can be no greater arrogance." The Secretary-General went on to demolish the argument that nuclear weapons and the strategy of deterrence have kept the peace. "If nuclear weapons are indeed peace-keepers, does it not follow that they ought to be acquired by every nation on earth? On the contrary, it is clear that to rely on nuclear deterrence is to accept a perpetual community of fear."

Of course world pressure on the nuclear powers grew. The Non-Proliferation Treaty came into existence in 1970, and the Anti-Ballistic Missile Treaty two years later. In 1987, the U.S. and the Soviet Union agreed to eliminate their intermediate-range nuclear weapons. Strategic Arms Limitation Talks took place; then with the fall of the Berlin Wall and the demise of the Soviet Union, START agreements were entered into to reduce the numbers of strategic (i.e., long-range) weapons. Short-range nuclear weapons, known as tactical or battlefield weapons, were cut back. The U.S. and Russia entered the Moscow Treaty of 2002, pledging to reduce their operationally deployed nuclear weapons to a maximum of 2,200 each by 2012. With the Cold War over, the public generally took the view that the nuclear arms race was finished, too. Nothing could be farther from the truth. While the total number of nuclear weapons had been cut from a high of about 65,000 at the height of the Cold war to more than 30,000 today, the nuclear weapons states have entrenched them in their military doctrines.

The nuclear weapons states have refused to enter comprehensive negotiations towards elimination of their nuclear arsenals. The U.S. and Russia still insist on maintaining about 2,000 strategic weapons each on constant alert status, meaning they could be fired on fifteen minutes' notice. The world faces immense danger from the policies of the powerful; the breakout of the new nuclear weapons states of India, Pakistan and Israel; and the possibility of still more states, such as North Korea and Iran, joining the nuclear club.

Nuclear War by Accident

The risks to humanity come not only from the possibility of nuclear warfare but also from accidents. There are many documented cases of the near use of nuclear weapons as a result of computer malfunctions.

Just past midnight on September 26, 1983, Lieutenant Colonel Stanislav Petrov was on duty as commander of an early warning bunker south of Moscow. Suddenly, computer alarms sounded, warning that an American missile from

Malmstrom Air Force Base in Montana was headed towards the Soviet Union. The team of 120 technicians and military officers looked to Petrov for a decision: to recommend immediately to Soviet leadership to counterattack or not? Petrov reasoned that a computer error had occurred, since the U.S. was not likely to launch just one missile if it were attacking the Soviet Union; it would launch many. But a few minutes later, another launch was detected, then more. Suddenly, a total of five missiles appeared to be flying towards the Soviet Union. The sound of the alarms was deafening. In front of Petrov, the word "Start" was flashing in bright lettering, the instruction to launch a massive counterstrike against the U.S. Petrov had only a couple of minutes to decide what to tell the Soviet leadership. He made his decision: he would trust his intuition and declare it a false alarm. If he were wrong, he realized that nuclear missiles from the U.S. would soon be exploding over the Soviet Union. As the minutes passed, everything remained quiet.

Petrov, by his calmness, prevented a worldwide nuclear war. Though he was congratulated by those around him, he said in subsequent interviews that he underwent intense questioning by his superiors. Because he had ignored computer warnings, he was no longer considered a reliable military officer and his once promising military career came to an end. He retired from the military to life as a pensioner. Petrov has said that he does not consider himself a hero, but many analysts consider the incident the closest the world has ever come to nuclear war. In 2004, in recognition of his actions, Petrov received the World Citizen Award, and the Australian Senate passed a motion to commend him.

What really was going on the night Petrov made his far-reaching decision? In the early 1980s, the Reagan administration labelled the Soviet Union the "evil empire" and started research on the Strategic Defense Initiative (known as Star Wars). The Soviets saw the U.S. government preparing for a first strike; in fact, the U.S. and NATO organized a military exercise that centred on using tactical nuclear weapons in Europe. On September 1, 1983 (three weeks before the Petrov incident), the Soviet military shot down a Korean passenger jet, killing all 269 people on board, including many Americans. Soon after, the KGB sent a flash message warning about a possible nuclear war. At the time, the Soviets had placed nine satellites in high elliptical orbit to scan the skies above U.S. missile fields. On the night of September 26, a Soviet satellite, Cosmos 1382, reached the highest point of its orbit, 32 km above the earth's surface. It is speculated that scattered high-altitude clouds over Malmstrom Air Force Base on that day (still daylight in Montana) reflected sunlight into the infrared sensors aboard the satellite, imitating the bright light given off by the hot gases in a missile's plume. It is possible that the sun lined up with the U.S. missile fields and the satellite to give spectacular reflections, which triggered the alarm in Petrov's centre. The next year, the Soviet Union started dedicating one early-warning satellite in geostationary orbit (positioned over the eastern Atlantic Ocean) to act as a backup to other satellites. This step guaranteed that U.S. missile fields could always be seen from two very different viewing angles, at least one of which would be free of reflections at any given moment.

Though nuclear proponents like to say that fail-safe improvements have been built into nuclear systems, there have nonetheless been other recorded near-accidents. A famous incident occurred in 1995. Russian warning radars detected a rocket rising out of the Norwegian Sea that appeared to be a U.S. submarine-launched Trident missile targeted at Moscow. The warning was relayed all the way up to President Yeltsin, who had only a few minutes to decide whether to launch a nuclear attack in response. Fortunately, Russian military officials determined that they had made an error in projecting the missile's trajectory: it was headed far out to sea, not targeted on Moscow. The rocket was American, but it was not a Trident missile. It was a scientific probe designed

to study the Northern Lights. The Russian government had
been told of the launch, but apparently "a mistake had been
made," and word never reached key military commanders.
Professor Lloyd J. Dumas of the University of Texas, who has
studied nuclear near-accidents, has listed 89 major publicly
reported nuclear arms–related accidents between 1950 and
1994. It is not known how many more near-accidents may
have gone unreported since.

Actual accidents in power plants have killed and imper-
iled the lives of countless people. The American chemical
company Union Carbide's facility in Bhopal, India, had a
well-constructed safety system, but on December 3, 1984,
a giant cloud of poisonous methyligocyante gas rose from
the plant and spread over the city. The toxic fumes killed at
least 3,800 people and injured more than 200,000. It took
20 years to disperse to victims the $470 million settlement
Union Carbide paid the government of India. On April 26,
1986, the Chernobyl nuclear power plant in Ukraine had
a meltdown as the result of an unforeseen combination of
flawed reactor design and human error. In addition to the 31
people killed, 135,000 people had to be evacuated because
of radioactive contamination. In 1995, the World Health
Organization linked 700 cases of thyroid cancer among
children to the Chernobyl accident. By 2000, 1,800 cases
of thyroid cancer were reported.

Human error happens in every area of life. Boredom
and stress lead humans to make mistakes. A monotonous job
can lead to boredom and a dangerous lack of attention. In a
stressful situation, it is easy to misinterpret what you see. The
use of alcohol or drugs to battle boredom or stress steps up
the risk of accident. Mistakes are constantly made in military
exercises and warfare. Four Canadian soldiers were killed
in "friendly fire" incidents in Afghanistan. "Friendly fire,"
the killing of your own or your allies' troops by accident, is
another of war's euphemisms. Mistakes with conventional
weapons, though tragic, are contained in their killing power.

Not so with nuclear weapons, the very effect of which is to kill massively. With nuclear weapons, there is no room for mistake; there is no learning curve.

As long as nuclear arms exist, the possibility of human error cannot be discounted. Leaders have to decide in an extremely short time whether a nuclear attack is truly in progress or simply a computer glitch. No leader should have to bear such a responsibility.

Nuclear Winter Nightmare

But irresponsibility and nuclear weapons go together, it seems. Although vested interests in the nuclear weapons industry have tried to discredit it, "nuclear winter" is set out in no less a source than the Encyclopedia Britannica as a possible outcome of nuclear warfare. The Britannica entry cites the 1983 TTAPS study (from the initials of the last names of scientists R.P.Turco, O.B.Toon, T.P.Ackerman, J.B. Pollack and Carl Sagan), which warned that even a limited nuclear war would cause death and injury to people on an unprecedented scale and would leave any remaining medical services with insoluble problems. People not immediately burned to death, blown apart or asphyxiated would find themselves in a nightmare world populated by the dead, dying and insane. Food, crops and land would be contaminated, water undrinkable. A similar United Nations study on nuclear winter shows that the indirect effects of a nuclear war could kill millions more through the breakdown of communications, transportation and financial systems, and all of this compounded by decreased temperatures, suppressed monsoons and increased ultraviolet radiation.

More than a decade of subsequent study by hundreds of researchers using progressively more sophisticated computer models essentially confirmed the original estimates with only minor revisions. These studies indicated that several hundred detonations, or fewer, would be sufficient to bring about nuclear winter. Even a small number of warheads aimed at petroleum refining and storage facilities would suffice.

Carl Sagan, who became famous as a popularizer of science, rebutted his critics:

> Some of what I describe is horrifying. I know, because it horrifies me. There is a tendency – psychiatrists call it "denial" – to put it out of our minds, not to think about it. But if we are to deal intelligently, wisely, with the nuclear arms race, then we must steel ourselves to contemplate the horrors of nuclear war.

He described a series of calculations pointing to an assault on human civilization from low land temperature and intense radioactivity lasting for months. The most rudimentary means for relieving vast human suffering would be unavailable. Immunity to disease would decline. "Epidemics and pandemics would be rampant, especially after the billion or so unburied bodies began to thaw." He said that perhaps the greatest surprise in the team's findings was that even small nuclear wars can have devastating climatic effects. Even a war in which only 100 megatons were exploded, low-yield airbursts over cities would ignite thousands of fires and the smoke from those fires would create intolerable damage. Sagan conceded that his analysis may be incomplete; however, nuclear war is not amenable to experimentation. "With billions of lives at stake, where does conservatism lie – in assuming that the results will be better than we calculate, or worse?"

> We have not yet experienced a global thermonuclear war – although on more than one occasion we have come tremulously close. I do not think our luck can hold forever. Men and machines are fallible, as recent events remind us. Fools and madmen do exist, and sometimes rise to power. Concentrating always

on the near future, we have ignored the long-term consequences of our actions. We have placed our civilization and our species in jeopardy.

In this Second Nuclear Age, nuclear proponents claim that low-yield nuclear weapons (e.g., a 5-kiloton warhead) will obviate all the massive repercussions of nuclear winter (even if the hypothesis is real). Thus, the U.S. is pressing for the development of a new low-yield nuclear "bunker-buster" to destroy deeply buried and hardened targets without causing massive collateral damage. The U.S. claims that this new nuclear weapon would be safer to use than current weapons, but the International Physicians for the Prevention of Nuclear War refuted this claim. The group's report on the medical consequences of exploding a nuclear bunker-buster says that even a very low-yield earth-penetrating weapon exploded in an urban environment would cause radioactive dirt and debris to fall out over several square kilometres. "A nuclear [bunker-buster] with a yield less than one-tenth of that of the nuclear weapons used on Hiroshima or Nagasaki could result in fatal doses of radiation to tens of thousands of victims." Casualties of this magnitude would overwhelm even the most effective medical care system. The physicians' findings are corroborated by the Union of Concerned Scientists, an independent alliance of more than 100,000 scientists committed to a cleaner environment and safer world. This group reported that "even a one-kiloton nuclear warhead that explodes 20 feet underground would eject about one million cubic feet of radioactive debris from a crater the size of Ground Zero at the World Trade Center."

The effort by nuclear advocates to introduce a new kind of nuclear weapon into the U.S. arsenal is part of a growing trend to lower the nuclear threshold and make the use of nuclear weapons more acceptable. Further, the use of such weapons would weaken existing restraints against their further proliferation or use and would cross a threshold that has been maintained since the bombing of Hiroshima and Nagasaki. It would almost certainly fuel a new cycle of global nuclear weapons proliferation, as other nations respond with their own new weapons.

Needed for What?

Numerous studies have examined the danger to humanity of any use of any nuclear weapon anywhere. Perhaps the best known is the report of the Canberra Commission on the Elimination of Nuclear Weapons, set up as an independent commission of 17 world experts by the government of Australia in 1995.

The Canberra Commission found that the destructiveness of nuclear weapons is immense and that any use would be catastrophic:

> The proposition that nuclear weapons can be retained in perpetuity and never used – accidentally or by decision – defies credibility. The only complete defence is the elimination of nuclear weapons and assurance that they will never be produced again.

The Commission made a compelling case for a nuclear weapons–free world, based on three main arguments.

First, the destructiveness of nuclear weapons is so great that they have no military utility against a comparably equipped opponent, other than by perpetuating the belief that they deter that opponent from using their nuclear weapons. They cannot be successful used against an opponent who has the power to retaliate in kind. Using nuclear weapons against a non-nuclear opponent is politically and morally indefensible. It would violate every aspect of humanitarian law.

Second, the indefinite deployment of nuclear weapons carries a high risk that they will eventually be used accidentally or inadvertently. The more states that acquire nuclear weapons the greater the risk a state will use them.

Third, the possession of nuclear weapons by some states stimulates other nations to acquire them, reducing the security of all. The proliferation of nuclear weapons jeopardizes every region of the world.

These rational arguments are lost on the nuclear planners, who have always been driven by an obsessive conviction that nuclear weapons are needed. *Needed for what?* They have been debunked as aids to security. The events of September 11, 2001, demolished that argument.

Needed to stop wars. The litany of regional and intramural wars since 1945 is a long one.

Needed to prevent World War III. How do we know? There is no historical evidence that the Soviet Union ever intended to invade and conquer Western Europe.

Needed by the powerful to keep smaller states from acquiring them. The crisis surrounding the Non-Proliferation Treaty described earlier shows that this is a lie. The truth is that the planners want nuclear weapons as instruments of power.

The defenders of nuclear weapons have put humanity in a trap. They have created instruments of massive death; they say these weapons are needed for peace; more nations try to acquire them, which raises the possibility of their use; any use will result in massive death. The only way out of this maze is for the public to stop being intimidated by military jargon and emphasize our common humanity. The lesson of the *hibakusha* must be taught anew.

6

Shooting Gallery
in the Heavens

Weapons of war, which for so long have despoiled the earth and caused massive human suffering, are about to enter the heavens. The strategy of conducting warfare "in, from and through space" as envisioned by the U.S. defence department and the Air Force is taking hold. The same factors – greed, power, arrogance – that have driven the nuclear arms race are at play in the coming weaponization of space. The forward march to a war in space is already setting back the earthly attempt to curb the proliferation of weapons of mass destruction. These facts must be grasped to understand what is going on in the world of weaponry.

For half a century, the co-operative and peaceful use of space has yielded immense benefits to humans worldwide. More than 750 active satellites are orbiting the earth, performing valuable work in communications, navigation, science and development, reconnaissance and weather forecasting. World operations are already heavily dependent on the peaceful use of satellites. Work that has been done by scientists on the International Space Station, the largest and most complex scientific project in history, will lead to discoveries in medicine, materials and fundamental science that will benefit people all over the world. Through research and technology, it will be an indispensable step in preparation for future human space exploration. Worldwide space industry revenues now total $110 billion a year, $40 billion of which goes to U.S. companies.

Space ought to be left to peaceful uses. There are already enough problems with space debris and the dangers it poses to weather and intelligence satellites travelling at 7.6 km per second, 30 times faster than the speed of a jet. But no. The Pentagon has put forward the Counterspace Operations Doctrine to develop weapons for "space superiority." An Air Force document called *Vision 20/20* projects the U.S. need for "full spectrum dominance," by which it means military control of land, sea, air and space. Air-launched anti-satellite missiles, space-based radio frequency energy weapons and launch platforms in orbit that hurl metal cylinders at earth targets with the force of a small nuclear weapon – all these will be the tools of future space wars. As General Lance Lord, Commander of U.S. Air Force Space Command, put it, "We must establish and maintain space superiority. Modern warfare demands it. Our nation expects it. Simply put, it's the American way of fighting." More than rhetoric is being expended here. The U.S. budget for 2006 contains more than $300 million for space weapons work. By 2008, the U.S. intends to test space-based kinetic-energy kill vehicles to destroy high-speed collision test targets in space.

There is an important distinction between the militarization and weaponization of space. Space has been militarized since the first reconnaissance and signals-collection satellites were lofted into orbit. But the multination satellites, operated by military units, all have one thing in common: they are benign. They perform highly important military and civilian functions, but none can attack other objects in space or damage any targets on the earth's surface.

This is about to change. The U.S. Ballistic Missile Defense program is the entry point for weapons in space. Although the first stage of work comprises only land- and sea-based interceptors, the Missile Defense Agency intends to eventually include space-based interceptors in its arsenal. This program, currently called the Space-Based Interceptor Test Bed, was granted $10 million by Congress for 2005. More money will be sought for additional experiments. The plan is for the Missile Defense Agency to orbit three to six interceptors for testing in 2012. The government has stated clearly its intention: "Over time, [the Missile Defense Agency's] acquisition approach will yield a fully integrated and layered [Ballistic Missile Defense System] capable of defeating ballistic missiles of all ranges in all phases of flight."

This work is leading to a new category of space weapons: chemical lasers, particle beams and military space planes. One of the problems with space-based lasers is that they would have to be fixed to a moving satellite. The laser and the object it is trying to hit would likely be travelling at different speeds, making it an almost impossible shot. This is why the technical experts are considering a particle-beam weapon, which would be able to fire beams of subatomic particles at a military target at near the speed of light. A particle-beam weapon would be able to generate power many times more destructive than that of any laser in development. The major obstacle to developing a functional particle-beam weapon is creating a power source that is light enough to put into space but that can produce millions of electron volts of power and tens of megawatts of beam power.

So there are plenty of technological problems still to be solved before space weapons are a reality. The timelines the scientists have set are likely wildly optimistic. It could be a decade or two before the first space weapon is operational. Also, there is the matter of cost. With the U.S. deficit now running so high and exacerbated by the cost of the Iraq war and measures to fight terrorism, Congress may well balk at providing the funding demanded by the space programmers.

Destabilizing Earthly Environment

The fact that space weapons appear to be a long way off is not the point. Rather, the concern is the U.S. starting down this road in its perpetual quest for superiority in every possible kind of weapon, which further destabilizes the military and political environment. One of the chief political architects of space weapons is Secretary of Defense Donald Rumsfeld, who previously chaired a congressionally mandated panel dealing with threats to U.S. satellites. The Rumsfeld Commission expressed a worst-case assumption that the weaponization of space is inevitable, that conflict will follow commerce in space as on the ground and that the U.S. must not wait to suffer a "space Pearl Harbor." A good many politicians and defence contractors appropriated this inflammatory language to make the case that U.S. space assets must be protected at all costs. The space warriors also conjured up the argument that, because of the unparalleled position of the U.S. in terrestrial warfare, weaker nations will carry out surprise attacks in space to neutralize its nuclear war-fighting advantage.

By seizing what is called the high ground in the control of space, the U.S. has begun to exercise pre-emptive and proactive strategies, such as planning for a space-based laser and other kill vehicles as part of the missile defence system. Further, the Pentagon's 2006 budget contained $60.9 million for an experimental XX5 spacecraft, whose "microsatellite payloads" could attack enemy satellites. Another $68 million is earmarked for a Near Field Infrared Experiment that would use infrared technology to disable a country's satellites. A key goal of Rumsfeld's policy is "to ensure our access to and use of space and to deny hostile exploitation of space to adversaries."

Both Russia and China have told the U.S. to stop talking this way and to get on with negotiations for a new space treaty that would shut off any weapons in space. But for the last several years, the U.S. has, virtually alone, blocked attempts at the Conference on Disarmament in Geneva to start such negotiations

Outer Space Treaty Peace Norm

There is only one principal treaty concerning weapons in space. The Outer Space Treaty of 1967 was concluded at a time before modern technological developments, when the United States and the Soviet Union, fearing the disastrous results of extending their military confrontation into space, joined with the rest of the international community in deciding that space must only be used for peaceful purposes. The treaty bans weapons of mass destruction from space and stipulates:

> The exploration and use of outer space...shall be carried out for the benefit and in the interests of all countries, irrespective of their degree of economic or scientific development, and shall be the province of all mankind ...[and] shall be guided by the principle of cooperation and mutual assistance.

Unfortunately, while the Outer Space Treaty prohibits weapons of mass destruction or any object carrying nuclear weapons from orbiting in space, it does not specifically prohibit other weapons. As Jonathan Dean of the Union of Concerned Scientists explains, "In practical terms, this means that nuclear weapons mounted on missiles may transit space and that weapons other than nuclear, chemical or biological may be placed in space orbit and used to attack targets in space or on earth." In short, countries are not at present prohibited from creating armed military bases on orbiting satellites.

An important norm has emerged during the life of the Outer Space Treaty for keeping space free of weapons and conflict and ensuring the peaceful use of space for the common good of humanity. Year after year, U.N. resolutions call for the prevention of an arms race in space. Though the U.S. has never supported these resolutions, virtually all other nations want to expand existing multilateral agreements to include an explicit prohibition against all weapons in space. In 2002, Russia and China introduced a draft treaty at the Conference on Disarmament that would bind parties to three basic obligations: 1. not to place weapons in orbit or celestial bodies; 2. not to resort to the threat or use of force against outer space objects; and 3. not to assist other states in activities prohibited by the treaty. The U.S. immediately countered by insisting that the Outer Space Treaty was adequate. In response, the Russian government repeated its concern that the absence of legal barriers to the placement of new kinds of weapons must be corrected. The Chinese government expressed concern about U.S. efforts to achieve "control of outer space." Chinese Ambassador Hu Xiado said, "It is no exaggeration to say that outer space would become the fourth battlefield after land, sea and air should we sit on our hands."

Whether the Russia-China version or some other, a new multilateral treaty is clearly needed to ensure that space is protected as the common heritage of humanity. Such a treaty is needed to complete, so to speak, the prohibition of nuclear weapons on earth. At present, the U.S. argument that it needs a ballistic missile defence system to protect itself against a nuclear attack is leading directly to the weaponization of space. In fact, some experts argue that it is the U.S. missile defence program that makes it imperative to develop a multilateral space treaty. The U.S., however, realizes that such a treaty would require it to greatly restrict its missile defences, which returns the spotlight onto doing something concrete to eliminate nuclear weapons.

How can a space weapons treaty be concluded when the most powerful state opposes it? All other states should go ahead and produce a new treaty, which would be followed by the creation of an international organization for common security in space. This, in turn, would raise the level of world public opinion to put pressure on the U.S. to join in. The rivals of the U.S. will say that this is too risky because as the U.S. goes ahead with the development of space weapons, other powerful states (Russia and China among them) would fall victim to the aggressiveness of U.S. policy to achieve full-spectrum dominance. Without the U.S. agreeing to participate in drafting a space weapons treaty, it will be almost impossible to get negotiations started. And without a space weapons treaty, the nuclear arms race on earth will roar on.

A Profound Human Problem

U.S. resistance to strengthening international law against new weaponry may seem puzzling until it is recalled that the Bush administration has made a specialty of undermining international law. The 2003 war in Iraq, abrogation of the Anti-Ballistic Missile Treaty, and rejection of the Comprehensive Test Ban Treaty, International Criminal Court and Kyoto Protocol on the environment all show a disdain not only for international law but also for co-operation. It is a short-sighted policy, in the view of Michael Krepon, president emeritus of the Henry L. Stimson Center in the U.S. and a space expert: "Although everybody loses if the heavens become a shooting gallery, no nation loses more than the United States, which is the primary beneficiary of satellites for military and commercial purposes." In short, the U.S. has more to lose than to gain by opening up space to anti-satellite and other space weapons. No country can expect to have a lasting monopoly on these weapons.

If the U.S. leads the way in testing and deploying new anti-satellite weapons, other states will surely follow suit because they would have too much to lose by allowing the Pentagon sole rights to space warfare. Moreover, weaponizing space would poison relations with China and

Russia, whose help is essential to stopping and reversing proliferation. Anti-Satellite weapons tests and deployments would likely reinforce Russia's hair-trigger nuclear posture, and China would likely step up its nuclear modernization program. This could stimulate India and Pakistan to further nuclear weapons development. Michael Krepon adds: "The fabric of international controls over weapons of mass destruction, which is being severely challenged by Iran's and North Korea's nuclear ambitions, could rip apart if the Bush Administration's interest in testing space and nuclear weapons is realized."

If the weaponization of space could be avoided during the Cold War, why can it not be today? The answer to this question is found in the ideology of military dominance. Globalization – the interdependent systems that make up the planet – requires what are called "rules of the road." With technology racing ahead to new frontiers, so too does space require "rules of the road." But if the arrogance of the major powers on earth cannot be overcome in the call for a nuclear weapons–free world, how will it be overcome in space? Instead of using the opportunity for earthly co-operation to save the heavens from weapons and then building on that co-operation to solve the nuclear weapons problem on earth, the U.S. is doing the exact opposite: its drive for space superiority is a further impediment to nations working together for a nuclear weapons–free world. In other words, the resolution to the problem of space weaponry must be found by speaking directly to the discordancies on earth. Since some nations think they have a right to possess nuclear weapons, which are capable of destroying life on Earth, they also likely think that they have a right to control the heavens. This is not a scientific problem; rather it is a profound human problem that must be addressed in all its ethical, economic and human security dimensions.

7

Nuclear Terrorism: An Elusive Threat

During his 24 years in the United States Senate, Sam Nunn acquired a reputation for military expertise that enabled his vote frequently to determine the direction of U.S. defence policy. A Democrat from Georgia, he was reputed to know more about NATO than any other member of Congress. He and Senator Richard Lugar, a Republican from Indiana, gave their names to the Nunn–Lugar Cooperative Threat Reduction Program, which provides assistance to Russia and the former Soviet republics for securing and destroying their excess nuclear, biological and chemical weapons. When Senator Nunn left the Senate in 1997, Georgia Tech named its school of international affairs after him. In 2000, he and Ted Turner, the philanthropist who founded CNN, started the Nuclear Threat Initiative, a private organization seeking to strengthen global security by reducing the risk of the use of nuclear, biological and chemical weapons. When Senator Nunn talks about the threat of nuclear terrorism, people listen. Here are three nuclear-related threats that he described to an international conference on nuclear security in March 2005:

Threat 1. A terrorist attack with a nuclear weapon

Under cover of darkness, terrorists slip into a nuclear research reactor in Belarus. Assisted by insiders, they take fifty kilograms of highly enriched uranium and head for a safe house that is equipped with machine tools, chemicals, bomb designs – everything necessary to turn a terrorist group into a nuclear power.

A few days later, intelligence agents discover the safe house, where they find machine tools with traces of highly enriched uranium – but no bomb. The combined security forces of many governments deploy to guard hundreds of ports and airports and thousands of miles of coastline. Yet the bomb moves through a border crossing – undetected by radiation sensors because it is shielded by a thin layer of lead. At midday in a city of several million people, the world suffers its first nuclear strike in sixty years.

Threat 2. A terrorist attack with a dirty bomb

A terrorist group with insider help acquires a dangerous quantity of cesium-137 from a medical facility. The terrorists use conventional explosives to incorporate the powdered cesium chloride into a "dirty bomb," and detonate it in the financial district of Paris or London or Tokyo or Beijing or Moscow or New York – dispersing the cesium isotope across a 60-square block area. The explosion kills a couple dozen people and millions evacuate the city in panic. Billions of dollars of real estate is declared uninhabitable. Cleanup is estimated to take years and cost additional billions.

Threat 3. A sharp increase in the number of nuclear weapons states

North Korea continues to turn its nuclear fuel into bomb-grade plutonium and manufacture nuclear weapons, and then suddenly tests a weapon – as India and Pakistan did in 1998. Nationalists in Japan and South Korea push their governments to develop nuclear weapons. China, in response, expands its own nuclear weapons arsenal and joins the U.S. and Russia by putting its weapons on a hair-trigger state of readiness. Iran continues playing cat and mouse, until it has developed enough highly enriched uranium to build several nuclear weapons.

As Iran and North Korea become nuclear weapons states, other nations re-examine their options. Before a decade passes, Egypt, South Korea, Japan, Saudi Arabia, Brazil, Argentina and Indonesia have become nuclear powers – provoking greater regional tensions, greater pressure on their nations to go nuclear, greater chance of nuclear accidents, and greater danger that weapons or materials could fall into terrorist hands. The Nuclear Non-Proliferation Treaty becomes an artifact of history.

Senator Nunn is not alone in saying the world is in a race between co-operation and catastrophe in trying to stop a terrorist group from exploding a nuclear bomb in a major city. Terrorist attacks against the mass transit systems of Madrid and London show the vulnerability of major cities. Restricting access to mass transit would defeat its very purpose: imagine trying to screen riders on the subways of New York City. Mohamed ElBaradei, Director General of the International Atomic Energy Agency, says the margin of security today is "thin and worrisome." This is because, with 40 countries now possessing the capability to produce nuclear weapons, the emergence of a nuclear black market and the clearly expressed desire of terrorists to acquire weapons of mass destruction have radically altered the security landscape.

Addressing the capacity of terrorists to obtain highly enriched uranium and improvise an explosive device with power equal to the Hiroshima bomb, the eminent physicist Dr. Frank von Hippel told a meeting at the U.N. in 2004: "Nothing could be simpler." In a long article in *The Atlantic* magazine, (January–February 2005) depicting the ways future terrorists would strike the U.S. (shopping malls, casinos, subways, theme parks), Richard Clarke, former White House counterterrorism chief, did not actually predict a terrorist nuclear attack, but he said,

> A nuclear attack on the United States is, along with the threat of a biological attack, the most frightening possibility to contemplate. Although developing and using even a crude nuclear weapon would be extremely difficult for terrorists, it is far from impossible, and the United States remains poorly prepared to defend against a nuclear attack.

The debate over whether it is "simple" or "difficult" for terrorists to commit a nuclear strike has a new urgency because of the World Trade Center attack. If the 9/11 terrorists had used a nuclear bomb at Ground Zero, hundreds of thousands of New Yorkers would have met the same fate as those in Hiroshima on August 6, 1945. U.S. security officials testified in Congress in 2005 that "it may only be a matter of time before Al-Quaida or other groups attempt to use chemical, biological, radiological or nuclear weapons." Senator Edward Kennedy of Massachusetts goes further: "If Al-Quaida can obtain or assemble a nuclear weapon, they will certainly use it – on New York or Washington, or any other major American city. The greatest danger we face in the days and weeks and months ahead is a nuclear 9/11, and we hope and pray that it is not already too late to prevent."

It is strange that this subject of immense importance does not receive more public attention. Beyond the immediate mass horror and lingering deaths from radiation, the casualties would include a mass deprivation of civil liberties, invasion of privacy, severely damaged world confidence in human security, and a breakdown in the world economy. The shock to international commerce, employment and travel would amount to billions and possibly trillions of dollars. In short, the consequences to the world of a terrorist nuclear attack would be staggering.

Buying, Stealing, Smuggling

The threat has been well analyzed in *Nuclear Terrorism: The Ultimate Preventable Catastrophe*, by Graham Allison, founding dean of Harvard's John F. Kennedy School of Government and former U.S. Assistant Secretary of Defense. He says the imminence of the threat stems from three sources.

First, thefts of weapons-usable material and attempts to steal nuclear weapons are proven facts. States have publicly confirmed 20 cases of nuclear material diversion, and more than 200 incidents involving illicit trafficking in nuclear materials have been documented over the past decade. In 1997, Russian General Alexander Ledbed, Assistant for National Security Affairs, acknowledged that 84 of some 132 special KGB "suitcase" nuclear weapons were not accounted for in Russia. Though the government tried to deny that this was so, a criminal case in 2003 revealed that a Russian businessman had been offering $750,000 for stolen weapons-grade plutonium to sell to a foreign client.

Second, if a terrorist group could buy or steal a small amount of uranium, it could produce an atomic bomb using information available on the Internet. A study by five former U.S. nuclear weapons designers concluded that a sophisticated terrorist group could design and build a workable nuclear bomb from stolen plutonium or highly enriched uranium, with potential yields in the kiloton range. Scientists have warned of the ease with which terrorists could, with parts from the open market, assemble a simple nuclear device in which two quantities of highly enriched uranium collide.

Third, smuggling nuclear material, even an assembled device, into any country, including the U.S., would not prove difficult, given that most cargo containers are not inspected. Less than 18 pounds of plutonium or 55 pounds of highly enriched uranium are sufficient to make a nuclear bomb; these materials circulate in civilian nuclear commerce by the ton.

Since al-Qaeda has vowed to kill more Americans – Osama bin Laden's spokesman has said, "We have the right to kill four million Americans" – a number of U.S. officials think that a nuclear terrorist attack on U.S. soil is inevitable. Graham Allison offers only the slightest of reservations: "In my own considered judgment, on the current path, a nuclear terrorist attack on America in the decade ahead is more likely than not." For his part, Senator Nunn says that he is not willing to concede inevitability. "But I do believe that unless we greatly elevate our effort and the speed of our response, we could face disaster."

The laxness in the world system was unwittingly exposed by A.Q. Khan, the father of Pakistan's nuclear bomb. In 2004, even nuclear experts were stunned by revelations that Khan surreptitiously ran a veritable "Wal-Mart of private sector proliferation," in the words of Mohamed ElBaradei. Khan, who is under house arrest in Pakistan, confessed to selling his country's most prized nuclear secrets, even though he received a presidential pardon. He is suspected of running a clandestine network for more than a decade, through which he sold technology and equipment to make nuclear weapons to Libya, Iran and North Korea. It is known that Khan sold material for nuclear centrifuges used to produce enriched uranium to Libya, which later renounced its possession of nuclear weapons. The Pakistan government says he also provided centrifuges to Iran. Did he also sell nuclear technology to Saudi Arabia and other Arab countries? Will one of his clients pass along nuclear technology and expertise to terrorist groups? These are questions opened up by the discovery of Khan's nuclear bazaar.

Nuclear Power Plant Risk

Almost 60 states currently operate or are constructing 440 nuclear power reactors, and at least 40 of these states possess the capability to build nuclear weapons. The nine nations that possess nuclear weapons collectively have enough highly enriched uranium and plutonium to build more than 100,000 additional nuclear weapons. The U.N.'s High-Level Panel on Threats, Challenges and Change has pointed out that, regardless of whether more states acquire nuclear weapons, grave risks are posed by the existence of large stockpiles of nuclear and radiological materials.

Making a nuclear weapon is not particularly difficult when the right nuclear fuels are present. A nuclear weapon requires either highly enriched uranium (HEU) or plutonium. A crude nuclear weapon would use 40 to 50 kg of HEU; a more sophisticated design would require 12 kg of HEU or 4 kg of plutonium. In the case of plutonium, this man-made element is created in reactors as a byproduct of nuclear fission. Plutonium can be used for either fuel or bombs. A nuclear explosion occurs when a chain reaction within a critical mass of fissile material, either HEU or plutonium, accelerates, becomes supercritical and releases nuclear energy. Because only a small amount of either substance is needed to build a bomb, terrorists could feasibly steal enough material to build one or more nuclear weapons.

While the low-grade uranium in many reactors cannot be used for bombs, it can be so used when enriched. The theft of HEU would be especially worrisome because it is relatively straightforward to make a bomb using this material.

Many countries possess significant stockpiles of plutonium and HEU, which, in some cases, are vulnerable to theft. HEU is used to fuel more than 100 research reactors worldwide in dozens of countries. Many of these facilities are in academic or industrial settings with inadequate security, making them even more attractive targets for terrorists seeking nuclear weapons materials. The U.S. National Academy of Sciences warns against the possibility of terrorists crashing a plane into a commercial nuclear plant, or using truck bombs in a ground assault, which would set off fires and disperse a large amount of radiation.

There is far more plutonium in civilian than military nuclear programs; since the advent of the nuclear age, 1,600 metric tons have been produced in reactors. With the amount of military plutonium shrinking, the amount of civilian plutonium produced in reactors is increasing rapidly, as the demand for nuclear power increases. Unless commercial reprocessing is halted, there will be nearly twice as much weapons-usable civilian plutonium as military plutonium by 2010. In fact, the nuclear power industry, recognizing that global energy demand will rise 60 per cent over the next 25 years, is about to introduce civilian plutonium as a commercial fuel on a massive scale on the world market. China, trying to curb the import of oil and gas and the use of coal, plans to build 40 new nuclear reactors in the next fifteen years to serve power needs on its booming eastern coastline.

Operating and construction costs of nuclear power plants have come down greatly since 1980. As a result, these plants have become more cost-competitive with plants fuelled by oil or natural gas. The economic advantage seems to be overcoming the continued fears of a nuclear accident, such as the one in Chernobyl, the risks of disposing and storing radioactive waste, and the possibility of terrorist attacks on nuclear plants. In this new economic environment, developing countries do not want tighter restrictions on their access to nuclear technologies and fuels, as the West is now trying to impose out of fear of nuclear weapons proliferation. As the 2005 NPT Review Conference showed, the only possibility of getting developing countries to co-operate to amend NPT rules is if the nuclear weapons states themselves show their sincerity in nuclear disarmament.

The awesome aspects of the vulnerability of the nuclear fuel cycle to nuclear terrorism are just becoming apparent. The Nuclear Control Institute, a U.S.-based advocacy centre for preventing nuclear non-proliferation and terrorism, which has long monitored the problem, says:

> The 21st century marks a turning point when more atom-bomb material enters civilian commerce than exists in all the world's nuclear weapons.

Is Multilateral Action Enough?

Multiple ideas, plans, strategies and laws are emerging from governments and the International Atomic Energy Agency (IAEA) to make nuclear fuels safe from terrorists. The Nunn-Lugar Cooperative Threat Reduction Program has been working since 1991 to secure and destroy weapons and materials in the former Soviet Union. This program helped Kazakhstan, Ukraine and Belarus get rid of all their nuclear weapons. Further, the G8 countries have committed $20 billion over ten years to eliminate some stockpiles of weapons of mass destruction in Russia, but the program is still struggling to move from pledge to action. The U.S. launched two programs: the U.S.-Russian Global Threat Reduction Initiative to remove and secure highly enriched uranium from research facilities around the globe, and the Proliferation Security Initiative to interdict the transfer of sensitive nuclear materials on the high seas. The Nuclear Threat Initiative, run by Senator Nunn, works with governments and non-governmental organizations to promote global awareness of the potential for catastrophic terrorism. The 1980 Convention on the Physical Protection of Nuclear Materials was amended in 2005 to tighten the protection of nuclear material against theft, smuggling and sabotage. Also in 2005, the Nuclear Terrorism Convention was opened at the U.N. for signature after seven years of negotiation. This convention defines acts of terrorism and strengthens the international framework to combat them. It requires those who threaten or commit such crimes to be extradited or prosecuted and provides for a broad range of mutual assistance obligations. The convention is good as far as it goes, but it stops well short of rendering it impossible for terrorists to obtain nuclear materials.

The most far-reaching action is Resolution 1540, unanimously adopted by the U.N. Security Council on April 28, 2004 from a draft text submitted by the U.S. The resolution requires all states to take measures to prevent non-state actors from acquiring or trafficking in nuclear, chemical and biological weapons and to prevent the spread of these weapons. The resolution, aimed squarely at preventing terrorists from acquiring nuclear materials, calls on all states to strengthen multilateral treaties to stop the proliferation of weapons of mass destruction. It was built on U.N. Resolution 1373, passed by the Security Council two weeks after the terrorist attacks of September 11, 2001, which required every state to freeze the financial assets of terrorists and their supporters, deny travel or safe haven to terrorists, prevent terrorist recruitment and weapons supply, and co-operate with other countries to share information and prosecute criminals. Resolution 1540 also requires states to establish export controls and other measures to prevent proliferation and to report back on the implementation of the resolution.

Though criticized for stepping outside the established treaties, Resolution 1540 has a particular advantage because it forces India, Pakistan and Israel – not members of the NPT – to enforce export controls. Pakistan, embarrassed by the revelations about A.Q. Khan, used the resolution to justify stricter measures. However, Resolution 1540 bypasses the safeguards and verification systems advocated by the IAEA as essential tools for nuclear security. The resolution is notably deficient, since it ignores nuclear disarmament and the inherent linkages between non-proliferation and genuine nuclear disarmament. No reference is made to the Thirteen Steps or even to the principles and objectives adopted by all the NPT parties when it was indefinitely extended in 1995.

The resolution carries forward the philosophy of the nuclear weapons states, who think that proliferation can be stopped without reference to their own responsibilities to help eliminate nuclear weapons. It projects the unfortunate message that nuclear weapons in the hands of those who have them is just fine but that no one else can have them. It ignores what should be the essence of a global strategy, which is to reduce the demand for nuclear weapons. Lacklustre disarmament by the nuclear weapons states not only weakens the diplomatic force of non-proliferation, but it also sends a message to other states that nuclear weapons are important for security. Thus, the hoarding of nuclear weapons by the powerful actually stimulates demand. Resolution 1540 attempts to choke off the supply of nuclear materials to terrorists, but as long as the demand stays high, the risk of nuclear terrorism also stays high.

The IAEA, which has long been in the business of detecting the transfer of nuclear materials (it carries out about 2,000 inspections at 600 facilities per year), launched a post-9/11 program of prevention, detection and response. It is as active as possible, but governments deny it the resources it needs to guarantee that all nuclear materials are safeguarded.

Since September 2001, the IAEA's Nuclear Security Fund
has received only $35 million from 26 countries, as well as
from the European Union and the Nuclear Threat Initiative.
This is a tiny fraction of what the nuclear weapons powers
spend every day to maintain their nuclear weapons. These
powers say they are serious about cutting off nuclear supplies to terrorists, but their financial and security priorities
belie that assurance. The 35 tons of potential bomb material secured in 2004 was just six per cent of the potentially
vulnerable nuclear material in Russia alone. If progress
continues at the same rate, it will take thirteen years to finish
the job in just the former Soviet Union. Access to sensitive sites, liability in the event of an accident and countless
other bureaucratic obstacles impede efforts to secure nuclear
materials. The IAEA has proven the effectiveness of its inspection programs in Iraq, Iran and North Korea, but still
the support it receives from the international community
as a whole is grudging.

So far, we have looked at the possibility of terrorists acquiring nuclear weapons to augment the havoc they could
wreak. What about the question of states using nuclear
weapons to fight terrorism? In other words, do the 9/11
attacks allow the nuclear weapons states to justify retaining their nuclear arsenals? Can nuclear weapons be used to
fight and destroy terrorism? These questions can be easily
answered. By its nature, terrorism is not susceptible to the
logic of nuclear deterrence. How could a nuclear weapon
be used with any semblance of morality or legality against
terrorists who live in urban centres and other communities
inhabited by countless civilians? The incineration of whole
populations can hardly be a civilized response to terrorism.
Besides, as 9/11 tragically showed, the terrorists who perpe-
trated that act had all been living for some time in the U.S.
Nuclear weapons are unusable in fighting terrorism.

Global Partnership Needs Equitability

Consistency and co-operation in applying strict laws and sanctions against either terrorists or states seeking to acquire nuclear weapons are the only ways to stop the cascade of proliferation. A global partnership is needed, requiring at least the co-operation of all the non-nuclear weapons states to apply strict multilateral control over the fuel cycle. But we cannot expect such co-operation while the nuclear powers are not willing to co-operate in implementing their side of the NPT bargain. Putting a moratorium on additional facilities for uranium enrichment and converting existing reactors to low-enriched uranium, thereby cutting off the wide distribution of this bomb-making material around the globe, cannot be done without the co-operation of the developing countries. Striving for stronger rules to achieve full compliance with NPT provisions requires the U.S. and Russia to visibly and steadily reduce their reliance on nuclear weapons.

But when it comes to demanding that the nuclear powers fulfill their obligations as key to cutting off the threat of nuclear terrorism, few mainstream critics appear willing to make this link. Graham Allison, in his important book, sets out "three no's" for denying terrorists access to nuclear weapons or materials: 1. no loose nukes (better standards of inspection); 2. no new nascent nukes (no new national production facilities for enriching uranium or reprocessing plutonium); and 3. no new nuclear weapons states (drawing a line after the current eight: the U.S., Russia, the U.K., France, China, India, Pakistan and Israel). He follows this up with "seven yeses": 1. making the prevention of nuclear terrorism an absolute national priority; 2. fighting a strategically focused war on terrorism; 3. conducting a humble foreign policy; 4. building a global alliance against nuclear terrorism; 5. creating the intelligence capabilities required for success in the war on nuclear terrorism; 6. dealing with "dirty" bombs; and 7. constructing a multi-layered defence.

This list is certainly incomplete. It fails to recognize that a global alliance to fight terrorism requires that a new measure of equitability be introduced into world affairs. Terrorism will not be defeated by "war," but by the full application of all the human rights enshrined in the Universal Declaration of Human Rights and the international covenants. Programs to promote economic and social justice and lessen ethnic and religious discrimination are needed to prevent violence from breaking out. Just as terrorism itself cannot be adequately curbed without addressing its root causes, which are systemic injustices in the world, so too nuclear terrorism cannot be eliminated without addressing the hegemony that the nuclear powers exercise over other states. As long as the nuclear powers retain their arsenals, the global alliance needed to head off nuclear terrorism will remain elusive.

8

The "Silent Tsunami"

When the world's most powerful earthquake in more than 40 years struck deep under the Indian Ocean on December 26, 2004, triggering a massive tsunami, whole villages, seaside communities and holiday resorts in 11 countries were obliterated. About 228,000 people were killed and two million survivors lost their homes, livelihoods and family members. Governments, private agencies and the public rushed to help the victims of what U.N. Secretary-General Kofi Annan called "an unprecedented global catastrophe."

It was heartbreaking to see the images of bloated corpses, traumatized children, wrecked buildings, frantic rescue workers and countless hands outstretched for food and water. A wave of compassion swept around the world and donations poured in. Water and sanitation projects for Indonesia. Hygiene kits and a health institute to train volunteers in psychosocial counselling in India. Temporary shelters in Sri Lanka. Aid groups did an admirable job saving as many lives as possible and providing survivors with the basic necessities – food, water, clothing, shelter, and medical care. Quick action prevented major outbreaks of waterborne disease that could have doubled the death toll from the disaster. Six months after the catastrophe, hundreds of thousands of people remained homeless. The tsunami was truly an earth-shattering experience.

Is there any lesson here about nuclear weapons? At first glance, it may seem not. After all, the earthquake happened far beneath the surface of the earth. While tsunami warning systems were sadly lacking in that part of the world, the primary cause of the suffering was an act of nature, far beyond human control. Earthquakes, avalanches, floods, hurricanes – all these terrors seem part of our planetary system. But on the human journey through time, we have learned to cope with the ravages of nature to some degree. In this instance, with millions made homeless and desperate for life-sustaining materials, the suffering of the survivors was immense. Yet much physical infrastructure remained in place: planes with relief supplies could land at airports, trucks could carry food and water along roads, medical personnel were on hand. The situation was terrible, but survival was possible.

The lesson we ought to draw from this experience is that governments and civil society must avert the still worse catastrophe that a nuclear weapons attack would set off. The *hibakusha* of Hiroshima and Nagasaki know the human consequences of a nuclear attack. The result of such an act would be the destruction of the very infrastructure required to help survivors. Only through luck – or is it the hand of God? – have we been able to escape a nuclear explosion through design or accident. We can do little to curb the awesome powers of nature, but we can and must do much more to curb the destructive power of nuclear weapons. We must wake up to the total calamity that would result from a nuclear war and realize that the human community will not be able to cope with such a human-made disaster. The tsunami warns us that every day that humanity tolerates nuclear weapons, we are one day closer to ultimate disaster.

Poverty: A Security Issue

The tsunami was also a vivid reminder of the complexities of the human security agenda. Though the Cold War is over, a new age of anxiety has arisen from the interplay of transborder problems. Among them are endemic poverty, convulsive economic transitions that lead to inequality and high unemployment, international crime, the spread of deadly armaments, large-scale population movements, recurring natural disasters, ecosystem breakdown, new and resurgent communicable diseases and increasing competition over land and other natural resources, particularly oil. These "problems without passports" affect the lives of people everywhere and are likely to worsen in the years ahead. They cannot be resolved by increasing military expenditures.

These problems, which make the lives of the most vulnerable so miserable, come to their apex in the issue of poverty. More that one billion people in the world live on less than one dollar a day. Another 2.7 billion struggle to survive on less than two dollars per day in the face of chronic hunger, disease and environmental hazards. Every year, 11 million children under the age of five die, the vast majority from completely preventable causes such as malaria, diarrhea and pneumonia. They die in anonymity. This is truly a "silent tsunami." Dr. Jeffrey Sachs, Coordinator of the U.N. Millennium Goals, the U.N. plan to halve poverty by 2015, says that the silent tsunami of malaria kills as many people in Africa every month as died in the December 26 tsunami. He says that every morning our newspapers should report: "More than 20,000 people perished yesterday of extreme poverty." How is this possible? The poor die in hospital wards that lack drugs, in villages that lack anti-malarial bed nets, in houses that lack safe drinking water. They die namelessly, without public comment. Sadly, such stories rarely get written.

Here are the basic facts of the roots and manifestations of the poverty affecting more than one-third of the world that ought to be in the daily headlines.

Health
- Every year, six million children die from malnutrition before their fifth birthday.
- More than 50 per cent of Africans suffer from waterborne diseases, such as cholera and infant diarrhea.
- Every day, HIV/AIDS kills 6,000 people, and another 8,200 people are infected.
- Every 30 seconds, an African child dies of malaria, which amounts to more than one million child deaths a year.
- Each year, approximately 300 to 500 million people are infected with malaria. Approximately three million people die as a result.
- Tuberculosis is the leading AIDS-related killer, and in some parts of Africa 75 per cent of people with HIV also have TB.

Hunger
- More than 800 million people go to bed hungry every day; 300 million of these are children.
- Of these 300 million children, only 8 per cent are victims of famine or other emergency situations. More than 90 per cent suffer long-term malnourishment and micronutrient deficiency.
- Every 3.6 seconds, another person dies of starvation, and the large majority of these are children under the age of 5.

Water
- At least 2.6 billion people – more than 40 per cent of the world's population – do not have basic sanitation, and more than one billion people still use unsafe sources of drinking water.
- Four out of every ten people in the world do not even have access to a latrine.
- Five million people, mostly children, die each year from waterborne diseases.

Agriculture
- In 1960, Africa was a net exporter of food; today, the continent imports one third of its grain.
- More than 40 per cent of Africans cannot obtain sufficient food each day.
- Declining soil fertility, land degradation and the AIDS pandemic in Africa have led to a 23 per cent decrease in food production per capita in the last 25 years, even though population has increased dramatically.
- For the African farmer, conventional fertilizers cost two to six times more than the world market price.

The devastating effect of poverty on women
- More than 80 per cent of farmers in Africa are women.
- More than 40 per cent of women in Africa do not have access to basic education.
- If a girl is educated for six years or more, as an adult her prenatal care, postnatal care and childbirth survival rates will dramatically and consistently improve.
- Educated mothers immunize their children 50 per cent more often than mothers who are not educated.
- AIDS spreads twice as quickly among uneducated girls than among girls who have even some schooling.

• The children of a woman with five years of primary school education have a survival rate 40 per cent higher than children of women with no education.

• A woman living in sub-Saharan Africa has a 1 in 16 chance of dying in pregnancy. This compares with a 1 in 3,700 risk for a woman in North America.

• Almost half of the births in developing countries take place without the help of a skilled birth attendant.

All these problems have a common denominator: poverty. Pneumonia, diarrhea, malnutrition and malaria may be the killers, but it is persistent, deep-seated poverty that cuts short so many lives. In diplomatic parlance, these problems are often called the North-South imbalance, by which is meant that the two billion people in the North have access to and control over about three quarters of the wealth of the world while the four billion people in the South make do with only one quarter of the world's wealth. The enormous gap between rich and poor in the world produces political instability as well as human suffering. Poverty used to be considered a marginal problem, something that could perhaps be railed against morally, but political thinking is changing as a result of September 11. This is not to say that poverty causes terrorism; it doesn't. But, as the Worldwatch Institute, which monitors sustainable development trends, points out:

> Severe social, economic and environmental problems – particularly if mixed with festering political grievances – can radicalize societies and may even bring about state failure. Dysfunctional, fragile and violence-prone, so-called failed states are breeding grounds of despair and chronic instability, where warlords, criminal networks, or extremist groups are able to exploit a vacuum of governance and legitimacy.

Kofi Annan puts the issue this way:

> We now see, with chilling clarity, that a world where many millions of people endure brutal oppression

and extreme misery will never be fully secure, even for its most privileged inhabitants.

The Stingy Rich

Overcoming what divides increasingly disparate communities, cultures and nations and dramatically improving international co-operation are gigantic tasks. Kofi Annan challenged nations to do this when he introduced the Millennium Development Goals in 2000. The Goals included eradicating extreme poverty and attaining universal primary education by 2015, reducing child mortality, improving maternal health, combatting HIV/AIDS, malaria and other diseases, ensuring environmental stability, promoting gender equality and empowering women, and creating a global partnership for development. Such a program, he said, would cost $50 billion. The initial response of governments was mediocre, just as it has been to virtually every international campaign to help the poor and distressed of the world.

In 1970, former Canadian Prime Minister Lester B. Pearson led an international commission that set a target of 0.7 per cent of each developed country's gross national product to be devoted to Official Development Assistance. Thirty-five years later, the richest 22 countries allot on average just 0.25 per cent. The $78.6 billion they provide leaves a huge shortfall from the 0.7 per cent target. In the 1970s, global economic negotiations leading to more equitable use of the earth's resources were supposed to be held at the U.N., but the powerful countries killed them before they even started. In 1990, the U.N. World Summit on Children issued a high-minded declaration about meeting children's security needs, but little money was forthcoming. In 1992, at the Earth Summit in Rio de Janeiro, world leaders adopted Agenda 21, a document addressing every major development and environment problem, which carried a price tag of $625 billion. The developing countries said they would pay

$500 billion, but leaders in the developed world protested that their $125 billion share was unobtainable. A U.N. official incurred the wrath of developed country governments after the tsunami when he said that their first response to the calamity was "stingy." Annan smoothed over the ruffled feathers and the rich countries did subsequently pledge huge sums in aid. But even here they fell far short in their delivery. The Asia Development Bank said $7.7 billion was needed by India, Indonesia, the Maldives and Sri Lanka for rehabilitation and reconstruction, but three months later only $3.5 billion had been committed by donor countries and agencies, leaving a gap of $4.2 billion.

Aid to the developing world declined in the 1990s. Moreover, money actually moved from the South to the North. The U.N. reports that from 1994 to 2002, developing countries suffered a cumulative outflow of $560 billion as a result of trade law inequities, commodity pricing and debt servicing. The two principal international financial institutions, the International Monetary Fund and the World Bank, forced developing countries to adopt structural adjustment programs that reduced social services. In the past decade, dozens of countries have become poorer and devastating economic crises have thrown millions of families into poverty. The increasing inequality means that the benefits of global economic growth have not been evenly shared. The tsunami damage has exacerbated the ongoing needs of the developing world. For example, in East Asia alone, total infrastructure needs – rural roads, bridges, clean water and sanitation – amount to $1 trillion over the next five years, just to keep up with growing demand.

Zooming Military Expenditures

Large-scale disasters highlight the importance of establishing socially just priorities for government spending. Current priorities are all wrong. Military expenditures get the lion's share of government budgets, while the peace and human security programs starve. When the Cold War ended, the world community had a unique opportunity to make the 21st century one of peace and security. But the opportunity was squandered by the wars and conflict of the 1990s, and the terrorism of 9/11 resulted in a resurgence of worldwide militarism. Mikhail Gorbachev, former Soviet leader and a Nobel laureate for his work to end the Cold War peacefully, asks:

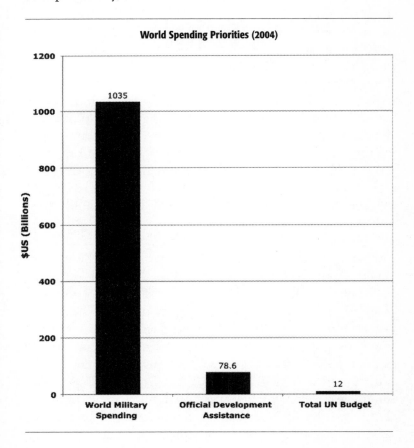

World Spending Priorities (2004)

Where has the "peace dividend" gone that we worked so hard for? Why have regional conflict and terrorism become so dominant in today's world? And why have we not made more progress on the Millennium Development Goals?

The answer to Gorbachev's plaintive questions lies in world military expenditures, which between 2002 and 2004 surged 20 per cent to $1.035 trillion. Military spending is now back up to peak Cold War levels. This is a scandal, an outrage, a theft from the poor of the world. Although the high-income countries account for only 16 per cent of world population, they account for 75 per cent of world military spending. This spending is 10 times higher than their Official Development Assistance. The Stockholm International Peace Research Institute, a leading source of military data, notes drily: "There is a large gap between what countries are prepared to allocate for military means to provide security and maintain their global and regional power status, on the one hand, and to alleviate poverty and economic development, on the other." In other words, the "peace dividend" from the end of the Cold War has been thrown out the window.

The United States accounts for nearly half of all world military expenditures. Of the U.S. total of $450 billion (some analysts put the figure at more than $500 billion), some $40 billion is spent on nuclear forces. This is $110 million every day spent on maintaining existing nuclear stocks and advancing concepts for new nuclear weapons. An audit by the Brookings Institute, which specializes in economic and foreign policy research, showed that between the dawn of the nuclear age and 1998, the U.S. spent a total of $5.8 trillion on nuclear forces. Such unwarranted military spending was, in the words of former U.S. President Dwight Eisenhower, a "theft" from the poor. Since secrecy pervades all the nuclear weapons states, it is virtually impossible to obtain an up-to-date global figure for nuclear weapons spending by all states, but a conservative estimate is at least $12 trillion. The amount of true human security – education facilities, health care systems, water and sanitation plants, housing, social services – that could have been obtained for even a fraction of that sum staggers the imagination.

Visualizing the Cost of Nuclear Weapons

Distributed evenly to everyone living in the United States at the start of 1998, the total estimated cost of nuclear weapons equals $21,646 per person. Represented as bricks of new $1 bills (such as one can obtain at a bank, bound at $200 to the inch) stacked on top of one another, $5,821,027,000,000 would stretch 459,361 miles (739,117 kilometers), to the Moon and nearly back. If $1 was counted off every second, it would take almost 12 days to reach $1 million, nearly 32 years to reach $1 billion, 31,709 years to reach $1 trillion, and about 184,579 years to tally the actual and anticipated costs of nuclear weapons. Laid end to end, bricks of $1 bills equivalent to the sum actually expended on U.S. nuclear weapons since 1940 ($5,481,083,000,000) would encircle the Earth at the Equator almost 105 times, making a wall more than 8.7 feet (2.7 meters) high.

From *Atomic Audit: The Costs and Consequences of U.S. Nuclear Weapons since 1940,*
Stephen I. Schwartz (ed.), Brookings Institution Press, Washington, D.C. 1998, p. 6.
(Used with permission.)

Governments are mean, short-sighted and stingy when dealing with the problems of human security, but they are profligate in preparing for and executing war. A few developing countries themselves, e.g. Burundi, Eritrea and Pakistan, have terrible priorities: they spend more on their own armed forces than they do on the people's education and health needs. But the most grievous offenders are the rich countries. The Group of Eight (G8), the richest and most powerful nations on earth, maintain nearly all the nuclear weapons in the world, account for most of the world's spending on the military and are the principal arms traders, but are cheapskates when it comes to providing aid to the poor. It is time to expose the duplicity of these self-appointed directors of the world. The G8 includes the U.S., the U.K., France and Russia, which all possess nuclear weapons; and

Germany, Japan, Italy and Canada, which support the nuclear powers. Together, the G8

- holds 97 per cent of all nuclear weapons,
- makes 75 per cent of annual world military expenditures,
- accounts for 87 per cent of the $40 billion in annual weapons trade, and
- provides only 0.22 per cent of their gross domestic product (GDP) in Official Development Assistance.

The G8 countries are undermining the rule of law by retaining nuclear weapons and sheltering under the nuclear umbrella. They are short-sighted and pushing the world towards even more economic, social and environmental disruption. Yet these drivers of the world economy have the greatest responsibility of any nation to lead the world towards equitable solutions for sustainable development.

At their 2005 summit in Gleneagles, Scotland, the G8 leaders took great credit for boosting aid to Africa by an additional $25 billion by 2010, but pointedly refused to make an overall commitment to reaching the target of 0.7 per cent of GDP by 2015. The weekend before the G8 meeting, the rock stars Bob Geldof and Bono produced 22 hours of live broadcasts from simultaneous rock concerts in London, Paris, Berlin, Rome, Philadelphia, Tokyo, Johannesburg, Moscow, Barrie (Canada) and Cornwall, England. It was estimated that up to two billion people heard or saw the "Live 8" concert extravaganza to raise awareness of poverty in Africa. The intention was to pressure the eight world leaders in taking unprecedented action. Geldof said that "the greatest concert ever" gave the G8 leaders "the largest mandate for action in history." Kofi Annan added his voice, appealing to the G8 for increased development aid, wider and deeper debt relief and a trade deal giving developing countries a real chance to compete on a level global playing field. The spectacular outpouring of public support for aid to Africa doubtless pushed the G8 leaders at least to make the $25 billion commitment, but that amount is equivalent to only 3.3 per cent of the G8's annual military expenditures. The leaders also committed themselves to making low-cost AIDS treatment accessible to all and for future trade talks to consider eliminating agriculture subsidies, which discriminate against developing countries.

Jeffrey Sachs criticizes the U.S. for neglecting the deeper causes of global instability in the war on terrorism.

> The nearly $500 billion that the U.S. will spend this year on the military will never buy lasting peace if the U.S. continues to spend only one-thirtieth of that, around $16 billion, to address the plight of the poorest of the poor, whose societies are destabilized by extreme poverty. The $16 billion represents 0.15 per cent of U.S. income, just 15 cents on every $100 of our national income.

Weapons or Water? Guns or Bread?

Sachs' remedy for poverty relies on a simple argument: more money. He led a team of 265 of the world's leading development experts that produced a report, *Investing in Development*, showing governments how to achieve the Millennium Development Goals by 2015. The plan is based on targeting investments in essential public services such as health, education and infrastructure to make communities less vulnerable to disasters and to such hardships as disease, hunger and environmental degradation.

One Trillion Dollars

World military spending in 2004 exceeded $1 trillion (U.S.). What is $1 trillion equal to?

– A stack of $1000 bills 109 km high.

– The entire output of the Canadian economy in 2004.

– One half of the annual health care costs of the U.S.

– The annual income of the Forbes 400 list of America's most wealthy.

Sources: *United Nations Trade and Development Organization; CIA World Factbook.*

The Sachs' report calls for bold action to lift 500 million people out of poverty, with a great proportion of the improvements to be made in Africa. Even achieving the Millennium Goals is only a midpoint on the journey to ending absolute poverty. It will be a long time before development assistance becomes unnecessary. So, for the near future, the Millennium Development Goals should form a centrepiece of the world's security agenda. Kofi Annan's approach is reasoned and appealing. To launch the debate at the Summit of World Leaders marking the 60th anniversary of the U.N. in 2005, he issued a comprehensive document, *In Larger Freedom: Towards Development, Security and Human Rights for All,* which began with these words:

Five years into the new millennium, we have it in our power to pass on to our children a brighter inheritance than that bequeathed to any previous generation. We can halve global poverty and halt the spread of major known diseases in the next 10 years. We can reduce the prevalence of violent conflict and terrorism. We can increase respect for human dignity in every land. And we can forge a set of updated international institutions to help humanity achieve these noble goals. If we act boldly – and if we act together – we can make people everywhere more secure, more prosperous and better able to enjoy their fundamental human rights.

For more than two decades, the United Nations has fostered a better understanding of how human security can be strengthened by the simultaneous application of both disarmament and development. As steps towards disarmament are taken, more funds should be released for economic and social development; as development occurs, it should reduce tensions and make significant disarmament measures tenable. Taken together, disarmament, development and security form a "dynamic triangular relationship." The U.S. boycotted the very conference that identified that relationship – the 1987 International Conference on the Relationship Between Disarmament and Development – on the grounds that there is no such relationship.

Very few states have seized on these mutually reinforcing steps for security, as burgeoning military expenditures and shrinking pools of capital for the alleviation of poverty attest. Proponents of social justice policies are marginalized in the media and public debates. The intense focus on terrorism, weapons of mass destruction and the war in Iraq have diverted high-level political attention away from financing sustainable development. The enormous sums spent on nuclear weapons should be diverted to human needs. Public investment in solutions to waterborne diseases actually shrank over the past decade, when nations piled increasing amounts of money into nuclear weapons. To meet clean water needs alone, 275,000 people must be hooked up to water sources every day until 2015. Halving those without access to water and sanitation would require a minimum of $10 billion per year. The nuclear weapons states spend many times that amount every year maintaining their nuclear arsenals.

Weapons or water? Guns or bread? This is the stark choice facing humanity. Yet, governments are mired in inertia, seemingly incapable of effecting political priorities to stop the race to destruction and promote a life of basic decency for all.

Society must examine the economic consequences of nuclear weapons much more. This could be stimulated by examining the morality and legality of nuclear weapons, to which I now turn.

PART III

The Moral and Legal Case Against Nuclear Weapons

9

Nuclear Weapons Are Anti-Human

On October 2, 2002, Ardeth Platte and two other Dominican sisters, Carol Gilbert and Jackie Hudson, wearing suits bearing the initials CWIT (Citizen Weapon Inspection Team), snipped the locks on the gates of two fences in a farmer's field in northeastern Colorado. They walked to a missile silo cover housing a 355-kiloton Minuteman III nuclear weapon, 20 times more powerful than the Hiroshima bomb, which can be triggered on fifteen minutes' notice. The women tapped on the rails with small hammers and poured baby bottles of their own blood onto the cement casing in a symbolic act of turning swords into ploughshares. With a crucifix, rosaries and prayer books, they prayed, sang hymns and sat down to await arrest, which came 40 minutes after their illegal entry. Here is how a judge described the scene:

> Defendants' actions triggered a swift response. Air Force security personnel were diverted from training exercises and arrived at the missile site in several armed vehicles. They crashed through the partially open outer gate because they were not sure it was safe to exit the vehicles. As they approached further, they observed Defendants standing on top of the

concrete blast door carrying black bags. The three women appeared to be praying and singing. Because the security personnel could not immediately discern what was in the black bags, they summoned a helicopter and explosives experts. Neighbouring Highway 14 was closed in both directions. Defendants were surrounded by officers with guns drawn. Continuing to sing and pray, the three women announced that they were peaceful and surrendered with their hands in the air.

Altogether, 20 to 30 security personnel arrived from the military police, the sheriff's office, the Office of Special Investigations, the FBI and the Explosive Ordnance Device team at the base. The U.S. government pressed sabotage charges and the three women were convicted. They lost their appeal.

Sister Ardeth said at her trial:

Sisters Carol, Jackie and I believe that we had a responsibility to inspect, expose and symbolically disarm this weapon of mass destruction to avert a crime of our government and uphold the laws of the United States, not break them. Don't people claim today that the citizens of Germany should have blocked the trains carrying people to the crematoriums, dismantled the ovens, or done something to stop the mass murder of people by Hitler? How will future generations judge us all?

In the course of writing this book, I went to the federal penitentiary in Danbury, Connecticut, to visit Sister Ardeth Platte, who was sentenced to three-and-a-half years for her protest against nuclear weapons.

Wearing a drab olive-grey prison uniform, Sister Ardeth greeted me with a big smile. We sat at a small table in the recreation room, with a guard about 20 feet away. I asked her for a message for the people I reach in my work. "We are all one creation," she said. "If we do not stop violence and care for one another, we are all diminished. Nuclear weapons are the ultimate evil. We must hold the U.S. accountable for dismantling nuclear weapons. They are instruments of murder."

She told me about the reflection group she has organized with other women prisoners. They read Scripture and current affairs books together. "I do a lot of contemplation. I want to give my life to God for nuclear disarmament. I find that being in prison is a special ministry. I never regret imprisonment. It's a sacrifice, but I want to make the time sacred." She spoke calmly and seemed to be at peace with herself. Fifty years a nun, Sister Ardeth has a long record as a social activist; she participated in sit-ins and marches against the Vietnam War. "We must stop teaching our young men in the military to kill," she said. "It's so barbarous."

As a public official for so many years, I cannot counsel breaking the law. But does that mean I must oppose non-violent civil disobedience for a cause aimed at curing the world of evil? The fact is that it is governments who are breaking the limitation and proportionality laws of humanitarian warfare by entrenching nuclear weapons in their military doctrines. The nuclear weapons states, of which the U.S. is by far the most powerful, are doing exactly that. The International Court of Justice has ruled that the threat or use of nuclear weapons is generally illegal and has stated clearly that nations must conclude negotiations for total elimination of those weapons. So the actions taken by Sister Ardeth and her colleagues, illegal as they may be, are designed to address an infinitely greater illegality, the threat to kill massively. When the Second Vatican Council said in the *Pastoral Constitution on the Church in the Modern World* that the courage of those who openly and fearlessly resist laws designed for the extermination of peoples "merits supreme commendation," the Council may well have had people like Sister Ardeth in mind.

Some, of course, consider these nuns and others, such as the Berrigan priest brothers, Dan and Philip, who also went to jail for protesting warfare, as mere idealists who get in the way of national policies. But non-violent civil disobedience as practised by Mahatma Gandhi and Martin Luther King achieves impressive results. Who knows where self-sacrificing protests against the evil of nuclear weapons will lead? Without a doubt, radical change in national and international politics is essential to reverse present trends in the war culture. The poor and vulnerable of the world and those being killed in the endless parade of wars need someone to speak up on their behalf. Sister Ardeth Platte is speaking up.

The Voice of Religion

Though the voice of religion has been raised against nuclear weapons, the volume of that voice needs to be turned up in light of the developments of the Second Nuclear Age. The religions of the world need to proclaim that nuclear weapons and human security cannot co-exist.

In 1983, the World Council of Churches, a fellowship of 342 denominations from virtually all Christian traditions in more than 120 countries, rejected the doctrine of nuclear deterrence and unequivocally declared:

> That the production and deployment as well as the use of nuclear weapons are a crime against humanity and that such activities must be condemned on ethical and theological grounds.

The Canadian Council of Churches, a community of 19 denominations, stated in 1998:

> The willingness, indeed the intent, to launch a nuclear attack in certain circumstances bespeaks spiritual and moral bankruptcy.... Nuclear weapons do not, cannot, deliver security – they deliver only

insecurity and peril through their promise to annihilate that which is most precious, life itself and the global ecosystem upon which all life depends. Nuclear weapons have no moral legitimacy.

In 1999, more than 7,000 people from around the world gathered in Capetown, South Africa, for the Parliament of the World's Religions and issued *A Moral Call to Eliminate the Threat of Nuclear Weapons*, which states:

> The threat and use of nuclear weapons is incompatible with civilized norms, standards of morality and humanitarian law which prohibit the use of inhumane weapons and those with indiscriminate effects. We say that a peace based on terror, a peace based upon threats of inflicting annihilation and genocide upon whole populations, is a peace that is morally corrupting.

The next year, 21 top religious leaders in the United States, joined by 18 military professionals, proclaimed in a statement issued at the Washington National Cathedral:

> We deeply believe that the long-term reliance on nuclear weapons in the arsenals of the nuclear powers, and the ever-present danger of their acquisition by others, is morally untenable and militarily unjustifiable.... National security imperatives and ethical demands have converged to bring us to the necessity of outlawing and prohibiting nuclear weapons worldwide.

Jewish and Muslim voices have also been heard, as befitting the fact that all three revealed religions, Christianity, Judaism and Islam, have deep commitments to compassion, justice and peace.

The Central Conference of American Rabbis, founded in 1889 as the organized rabbinate of Reform Judaism, expressed its concern in 1982 about nuclear war in terms of Jewish traditions:

A "limited" one, would result in death, injury, and disease on a scale without precedent. Civil defense and medical treatment would be totally inadequate. Our traditions speak to us of Sakanat Nefashot, the danger of exposing ourselves to health hazards; Bal Tashchit, the abhorrence of willful destruction of the environment; and Yishuv Ha-arets, the betterment and guardianship of the earth.

In 2000, Muzammi H. Siddiqi, President of the Islamic Society of North America, called for a total ban on the production and testing of nuclear weapons: "Islam stands for peace and protection of all human beings and their environment. Islam is against any war in which the innocent and the non-combatants are made to suffer."

The Christian, Jewish and Islamic voices that have been heard on the issue of nuclear weapons are mostly from groups or individuals within the structures of those religions. The official structures themselves are silent, for the most part. Not so the Catholic Church.

Definitive Catholic teaching on nuclear deterrence is found in Vatican II and subsequent statements by Pope John Paul II. Vatican II taught:

> Any act of war aimed indiscriminately at the destruction of entire cities or of extensive areas along with their population is a crime against God and man himself. It merits unequivocal and unhesitating condemnation. (*Pastoral Constitution on the Church in the Modern World*, No. 80)

The *Catechism of the Catholic Church*, published in 1992 on the 30th anniversary of the opening of Vatican II, affirmed the permanent validity of moral law during armed conflict. It stated, "The mere fact that war has regrettably broken out does not mean that everything becomes licit between the warring parties." It warns against modern warfare with the opportunity it provides to commit crimes against God and man through the use of atomic, biological and chemical weapons. The Catechism also draws attention to "rigorous consideration" that must be given to claims of legitimate defence, stating: "The use of arms must not produce evils and disorders graver than the evil to be eliminated. The power of modern means of destruction weighs very heavily in evaluating this condition."

Though they elaborated their concern that a universal public authority be put in place to outlaw war, the fathers of Vatican II rather grudgingly accepted the strategy of nuclear deterrence. The accumulation of arms, they said, serves "as a deterrent to possible enemy attack." Thus "peace of a sort" is maintained, though the balance resulting from the arms race threatens to lead to war, not eliminate it. Pope John Paul II restated the Catholic position on nuclear deterrence in a message to the U.N. Second Special Session on Disarmament in 1982:

> In current conditions, "deterrence" based on balance, certainly not as an end in itself but as a step on the way towards a progressive disarmament, may still be judged morally acceptable. Nonetheless, in order to ensure peace, it is indispensable not to be satisfied with the minimum, which is always susceptible to the real danger of explosion.

In this statement, it is readily seen that deterrence, in order to be acceptable, must lead to disarmament measures. Consequently, deterrence as a single, permanent policy is not acceptable. The American bishops' 1983 *Pastoral Letter on War and Peace* took up this theme. Though the bishops expressed a strong "no" to nuclear war, declared that a nuclear response to a conventional attack is "morally unjustifiable," and were skeptical that any nuclear war could avoid the massive killing of civilians, they gave a "strictly conditioned moral acceptance of nuclear deterrence."

In a five-year follow-up to their letter, the bishops set out criteria to be met to continue morally justifiable deterrence. For example, the bishops said that, to be acceptable, nuclear deterrence could not be based on the direct targeting of urban populations. Also, the bishops opposed weapons combining size, accuracy and multiple warheads in a credible first-strike posture. A subsequent follow-up in 1993, *The Harvest of Justice Is Sown in Peace*, repeated that "nuclear deterrence may be justified only as a step on the way towards progressive disarmament." The bishops held that "security lies in the abolition of nuclear weapons and the strengthening of international law."

Gospel Call of Love

As bishops of the Church in the United States, it is incumbent on us to speak directly to the policies and actions of our nation.

We speak now out of love not only for those who would suffer and die as victims of nuclear violence, but also for those who would bear the terrible responsibility of unleashing these horrendous weapons.

We speak out of love for those suffering because of the medical effects in communities where these weapons are produced and are being tested.

We speak out of love for those deprived of the barest necessities because of the huge amount of available resources committed to the continued development and ongoing maintenance of nuclear weapons.

We speak out of love for both victims and the executioners, believing that "the whole law is fulfilled in one statement, namely, 'You shall love your neighbour as yourself'" (Gal. 5-14).

It is out of this love that we raise up our voices with those around the world in calling for an end to the reliance on nuclear deterrence and instead call upon the United States and the other nuclear weapons states to enter into a process leading to the complete elimination of these morally offensive weapons.

– From the statement prepared
by Pax Christi in 1998
and signed by 75 U.S. Catholic Bishops

As the 1990s progressed, it became clear that U.S. policy was not moving towards nuclear disarmament. Even before the arrival of the Bush administration in 2001, the U.S. rejected a no-first-use policy and adopted flexible targeting strategies to use nuclear weapons either pre-emptively or in response to chemical and biological weapon attacks. The Bush administration's Nuclear Posture Review explicated the maintenance of nuclear weapons for war-fighting strategies. In 1998, seeing the institutionalization of nuclear deterrence taking place, 75 U.S. Catholic bishops signed a statement criticizing the U.S. for moving beyond original nuclear deterrence policies "to which we grudgingly gave our moral approval in 1983." The bishops said they were painfully aware that many policy makers sincerely believe that possessing nuclear weapons is vital for national security. "We are convinced, though, that it is not. Instead, they make the world a more dangerous place."

> We cannot delay any longer. Nuclear deterrence as a national policy must be condemned as morally abhorrent because it is the excuse and justification for the continued possession and further development of these horrendous weapons.

In 1997, the Holy See's Permanent Representative at the United Nations, Archbishop Renato Martino, was moving in the same direction when he told the U.N. Committee on Disarmament:

> Nuclear weapons are incompatible with the peace we seek for the 21st century. They cannot be justified. They deserve condemnation. The preservation of the Non-Proliferation Treaty demands an unequivocal commitment to their abolition.... This is a moral challenge, a legal challenge and a political challenge. That multiple-based challenge must be met by the application of our humanity.

In his address the following year, Archbishop Martino said:

> The most perilous of all the old Cold War assumptions carried into the new age is the belief that the

strategy of nuclear deterrence is essential to a nation's security. Maintaining nuclear deterrence into the 21st century will not aid but impede peace. Nuclear deterrence prevents genuine nuclear disarmament. It maintains an unacceptable hegemony over non-nuclear development for the poorest half of the world's population. It is a fundamental obstacle to achieving a new age of global security.

The Holy See spokesman again called for "the abolition of nuclear weapons through a universal, non-discriminatory ban with inspection by a universal authority."

At the 2005 Non-Proliferation Treaty (NPT) Review Conference, the Holy See made it clear that nuclear deterrence, in the modern context, cannot claim any moral legitimacy. Archbishop Celestino Migliore, the current Permanent Representative of the Holy See at the U.N., stated:

> When the Holy See expressed its limited acceptance of nuclear deterrence during the Cold War, it was with the clearly stated condition that deterrence was only a step on the way towards progressive nuclear disarmament. The Holy See has never countenanced nuclear deterrence as a permanent measure, nor does it today when it is evident that nuclear deterrence drives the development of ever newer nuclear arms, thus preventing genuine nuclear disarmament.

Archbishop Migliore warned that the new threat of global terrorism must not be allowed to undermine the precepts of international humanitarian law. In addition, "nuclear weapons, even so-called 'low-yield' weapons, endanger the processes of life and can lead to extended conflict."

> Nuclear weapons assault life on the planet, they assault the planet itself, and in so doing they assault the process of the continuing development of the planet. The preservation of the Non-Proliferation

Treaty demands an unequivocal commitment to genuine nuclear disarmament.

Short of Pope Benedict XVI himself speaking, the Holy See's position is now clear: because the nuclear weapons states have decisively shown that they consider nuclear weapons permanent instruments in their military doctrine, the Holy See has withdrawn the limited acceptance it gave to nuclear weapons during the Cold War. In the eyes of the Catholic Church, nuclear weapons are evil and immoral and must be eliminated as a precondition to obtaining peace.

The Holy See's address was in harmony with a speech given by Robert F. Smylie of Religions for Peace during the presentations by non-governmental organizations to the conference. Religions for Peace includes members of Baha'i, Buddhism, Christianity, Confucianism, Hinduism, Islam, Judaism, Janism, Sikhism, Shinto, Traditionalist/Indigenous, Unitarianism and Zoroastrianism. The statement recalled that, for more than 30 years, the interfaith community has come together to advocate for an end to war and weaponry. "The majority of religious leaders have always promoted disarmament, peace and policies that promote human security."

Addressing Secular Culture

The voice of religion in addressing the immorality of nuclear weapons is clearly important. If religion does not speak out on the paramount moral issue of our time – the threat of the annihilation of humanity – how can we expect the political order to consider the morality of their decision making? But religion by itself cannot raise the level of public attention high enough to be effective. First, religions too frequently speak only from their denominational perspective; some ecumenical co-operation in joint statements has occurred, but there is no sustained follow-through to impress on lawmakers the widespread nature of moral concern. Second, the failure of all the major religious leaders of the world to work and speak together results in compartmentalization of morality, which further weakens religious perspective. Third, even a sustained high-level joint religious call for the end of nuclear weapons, while much better than we have at the moment, would still tend to be marginalized from mainstream secular culture.

It is secular, humanistic culture that we must address when driving home to the political order that the world can no longer tolerate nuclear weapons. Religion must speak forcefully. That would be a strong beginning to efforts aimed at raising issues of the morality of nuclear weapons. But it must do more. Religions must learn to work with secularists for the common good of preserving the planet. They must find a way to show that morality is not something added on to daily affairs; rather, morality must be a first principle in any discussion of nuclear weapons, since it speaks to the heart of the continuation of life. Once this essential truth is recognized, new coalitions of action become possible.

Sir Joseph Rotblat, one of the fathers of the atomic bomb, who resigned from the Manhattan Project in moral opposition to such enormous destruction, provided an example of the fusion of religious and secular language on the anti-human nature of nuclear weapons. For many years, he was President of the Pugwash Conferences on Science and World Affairs and won the Nobel Peace Prize in 1995. Now 97, Rotblat sent a message to the 2005 NPT Review Conference.

> Morality is at the core of the nuclear issue: are we going to base our world on a culture of peace or on a culture of violence? Nuclear weapons are fundamentally immoral: their action is indiscriminate, affecting civilians as well as military, innocents and aggressors alike, killing people alive now and generations as yet unborn. And the consequence of their use might be to bring the human race to an end.

All this makes nuclear weapons unacceptable instruments for maintaining peace in the world.

Rotblat then sealed his argument:

> How can we talk about a culture of peace if that peace is predicated on the existence of weapons of mass destruction? How can we persuade the young generation to cast aside the culture of violence when they know that it is on the threat of extreme violence that we rely for security?

This language transcends religion as such, yet is deeply moral. It is language that crosses all boundaries and becomes inextricably interwoven with all the processes of daily life. This language can resonate with politicians, who need to be able to relate to all segments of their constituencies.

Nuclear weapons and human security cannot co-exist on the planet. Nuclear weapons are anti-human. That is what the moral aspect of the discussion is all about. Humanitarian law has always recognized that limitation and proportionality must be respected in warfare. But the very point of a nuclear weapon is to kill massively; the killing and the poisonous radiation cannot be contained. As I showed in Chapter 5, the social and economic consequences of nuclear war in a world whose life-support systems are intimately interconnected would be catastrophic. The severe physical damage from blast, fire and radiation would be followed by the collapse of food production and distribution and even water supplies. The prospect of widespread starvation would confront huge masses of people. Rampant disease would follow the breakdown in health-care facilities. These immense brutalities would violate the universal norm of life: to go on living in a manner befitting a human being with the inherent right to life.

No civilization, no culture has ever denied this common foundation upon which all peoples stand. Leaving aside the massive suffering, which by itself ought to stir the consciences of the nuclear proponents, the entire question of human rights would be up-ended. The right to a social and international order, as set forth in the Universal Declaration of Human Rights, would be completely lost. The structures underpinning humanitarian law would be gone. Order would be inverted into disorder. What is the "self" that the proponents of nuclear use for "self-defence" supposed to mean? The only way to really uncover the hypocritical defence of nuclear weapons as instruments of self-defence is to focus on the overarching humanitarian question.

"Remember Your Humanity"

Here, then, is the problem which we present to you, stark and dreadful and inescapable: Shall we put an end to the human race; or shall mankind renounce war? People will not face this alternative because it is so difficult to abolish war.

Although an agreement to renounce nuclear weapons as part of a general reduction of armaments would not afford an ultimate solution, it would serve certain important purposes. First, any agreement between East and West is to the good in so far as it tends to diminish tension. Second, the abolition of thermo-nuclear weapons, if each side believed that the other had carried it out sincerely, would lessen the fear of a sudden attack in the style of Pearl Harbour, which at present keeps both sides in a state of nervous apprehension. We should, therefore, welcome such an agreement though only as a first step.

Most of us are not neutral in feeling, but, as human beings, we have to remember that, if the issues between East and West are to be decided in any manner that can give any possible satisfaction to anybody, whether Communist or anti-Communist, whether Asian or European or American, whether White or Black, then these issues must not be decided by war. We should wish this to be understood, both in the East and in the West.

There lies before us, if we choose, continual progress in happiness, knowledge, and wisdom. Shall we, instead, choose death, because we cannot forget our quarrels? We appeal as human beings to human beings: Remember your humanity, and forget the rest. If you can do so, the way lies open to a new Paradise; if you cannot, there lies before you the risk of universal death.

From the *Russell-Einstein Manifesto*
signed by Bertrand Russell and Albert Einstein,
July 9, 1955

The humanitarian question is of growing concern to scientists and technologists who see the fruit of their work turned into instruments of death. A code of conduct for scientists, strengthening their resistance to more advances in the technology of killing, can come about by this emphasizing the assault to life that nuclear weapons pose. This was, in fact, the stance Bertrand Russell and Albert Einstein, two of the leading intellectual figures of the 20th century, took when they signed the Russell-Einstein Manifesto in 1955, along with nine other scientists. Their scientific critique of nuclear weapons ended with the stirring words: "We appeal as human beings to human beings: Remember your humanity, and forget the rest."

It is empowering to note that the age of weapons of mass destruction arrived just at the time when the Universal Declaration on Human Rights and its follow-up instruments were being codified. Just when we have finally decided that every human, no matter the culture, religion, ideology or geography, has the right to life, we have perfected our ability to kill massively. The U.N.'s idea of a culture of peace leads us inevitably to the recognition that every human being has the right to peace – in fact, to the "sacred" right to peace, as is said in the early declarations on this subject. The gradual increase in humanity's understanding of itself will lead to societal condemnation of nuclear weapons when it is fully understood that such instruments of evil are a violation of life itself.

Many powerful words have been written to condemn nuclear weapons in the court of world opinion. Perhaps the words of George Kennan, a distinguished American diplomat who originated the U.S. policy of containment towards the former Soviet Union, will one day energize whole populaces:

> The readiness to use nuclear weapons against other human beings – against people we do not know, whom we have never seen, and whose guilt or innocence it is not for us to establish – and, in doing so, to place in jeopardy the natural structure upon which all civilization rests, as though the safety and

perceived interests of our own generation were more important than everything that has taken place or could take place in civilization: this is nothing less than a presumption, a blasphemy, an indignity – an indignity of monstrous dimensions – offered to God!

10

"Illegal in Any Circumstances Whatsoever"

The fundamental argument of this book is that nuclear weapons are immoral and illegal. They are a crime against humanity.

Though treated separately, the moral and legal arguments have a common basis in humanity's long understanding that indiscriminate destruction of life violates the humanitarian value of life itself. This concept, understood in every culture and region of the world, gave birth to the classical laws of warfare written by Hugo Grotius of Holland (1583–1645), the acknowledged father of the international law we know today. The humanitarian laws of war, which gradually came into force, established these principles:

- prohibition against unnecessary suffering;
- proportionality;
- discrimination between combatants and non-combatants;
- obligation to respect the territorial sovereignty of non-belligerent states;
- prohibition against genocide and crimes against humanity;

• prohibition against causing lasting and severe damage to the environment; and
• supremacy of human rights law.

Essentially, humanitarian law protects the rights of the human person in time of war. To state that these principles have been violated by war makers through the ages does not invalidate them; it only reminds us of the long journey humanity is on to find the mechanism to enforce these principles. The journey has clearly begun: the Geneva conventions, the Nuremburg Convention, the existence of the United Nations, the special tribunals on Yugoslavia and Rwanda and the new International Criminal Court have all added to the implementation of human rights. The modern understanding of the inherent nature of human rights reinforces the existing legal mechanisms that protect humans against the ravages of war.

Viewed in a historical context, humanity is making some progress towards codifying the customary and conventional laws of war. An international treaty prohibits the use and possession of biological weapons; another prohibits chemical weapons. But there is no treaty expressly forbidding the use of nuclear weapons. The Non-Proliferation Treaty (NPT) obliges states to negotiate nuclear disarmament, but it does not ban outright the possession of nuclear weapons and is silent on their legality. The five permanent members of the U.N. Security Council (the U.S., Russia, the U.K., France and China), the original five nuclear weapons states, have made sure that no treaty – so far – universally bans the threat or use of nuclear weapons. The Model Nuclear Weapons Convention has actually been tabled at the U.N. as a working document, which I will discuss later in the book. Before governments can start to seriously discuss such a treaty, the question of the legality – or illegality – of nuclear weapons must be clarified.

The World Court's Opinion

This clarification was precisely the object of the World Court Project, launched by three principal groups: the International Association of Lawyers Against Nuclear Arms, the International Physicians for the Prevention of Nuclear War, and the International Peace Bureau. In 1992, they set out to get an advisory opinion from the International Court of Justice on the legality of nuclear weapons. The Court (known as the World Court) is the principal judicial organ of the United Nations. Sitting at the Peace Palace in The Hague, it has a dual role: to settle legal disputes submitted to it by states in accordance with international law, and to give advisory opinions on legal questions referred to it by the U.N. The Court is composed of fifteen judges, including one from each of the five permanent members of the Security Council. The Court has jurisdiction in disputed cases only when the parties involved agree to it. Although its advisory opinions are not binding, they emanate from the highest legal authority in the world.

The World Court Project secured the co-operation of the Non-Aligned Movement to introduce into the U.N. General Assembly a resolution urgently asking the Court to render an advisory opinion on this question: "Is the threat or use of nuclear weapons in any circumstance permitted under international law?"

The three Western nuclear powers – the United States, the United Kingdom and France – fearing that a decision that nuclear weapons are illegal would undermine their basic military doctrine, began intensive lobbying against the resolution. Experienced diplomats said the extreme reaction of the three amounted to hysteria; the Non-Aligned Movement buckled and the resolution was withdrawn. But the next year, the resolution was re-introduced and passed. The Court set two weeks aside in 1995 for oral hearings. (It also considered a similar resolution submitted by the

World Health Organization (WHO) on the health and environmental effects of nuclear weapons, but later declined to answer that question on the grounds that the agency, which specializes in health issues, is not competent to put its question to the Court.)

The World Court Project case turned out to be the largest in the Court's history to that date. Of the 43 governments submitting written opinions, two thirds held that nuclear weapons were illegal under international law. Twenty-two nations, including Japan, Egypt, Australia and Indonesia, gave oral testimony, most expressing the view that nuclear weapons are illegal. The U.K., on the other hand, argued that it would be "profoundly destabilizing" to call into question the legal basis of the system of nuclear deterrence. The U.S. argued that nuclear deterrence has saved many millions of lives from the scourge of war during the past half century.

On July 8, 1996, the Court handed down its 34-page advisory opinion. The Court began by noting the unique characteristics of nuclear weapons, particularly their capacity to cause untold human suffering and their ability to cause damage for generations to come. While Article 2.4 of the U.N. charter prohibits the use of force, Article 51 permits self-defence and Article 42 authorizes military enforcement measures. The Court reaffirmed the cardinal principles of humanitarian law: to protect the civilian population, states must never use weapons that are incapable of distinguishing between civilian and military targets; it is prohibited to cause unnecessary suffering to combatants and, hence, states do not have unlimited freedom of choice of weapons. Even though nuclear weapons were invented after the established principles and rules of humanitarian law had come into existence, it cannot be concluded that humanitarian law does not apply to them.

The Court then addressed the various arguments it heard: one side held that recourse to nuclear weapons, regulated by the law of armed conflict, is not prohibited;

the other view held that, in view of the necessarily indiscriminate consequences of their use, nuclear weapons can never be compatible with humanitarian law and are therefore prohibited. The Court held that the use of such weapons seems "scarcely reconcilable" with respect for humanitarian law, but added that it could not conclude with certainty that use would contravene international law in every circumstance. The Court recognized the reality of the strategy of nuclear deterrence "to which an appreciable section of the international community has adhered for many years." Accordingly, in view of the present state of international law viewed as a whole, the Court "could not reach a definitive conclusion as to the legality or illegality of the use of nuclear weapons by a state in an extreme circumstance of self-defence, in which its very survival would be at stake." It said that international stability suffers from these divergent views, and it is important to put an end to this state of affairs: long-promised nuclear disarmament is the most appropriate means of achieving that result. Calling attention to Article VI of the NPT, the Court said nations are obliged "to achieve a precise result – nuclear disarmament in all its aspects." Nations must pursue negotiations in good faith. "Any realistic search for general and complete disarmament, especially nuclear disarmament, necessitates the cooperation of all States."

The Court combined two distinct elements into one key vote. One paragraph stated: "The threat or use of nuclear weapons would generally be contrary to the rules of international law applicable in armed conflict, and in particular the principles and rules of humanitarian law." The next sentence said, "The Court cannot conclude definitively whether the threat or use of nuclear weapons would be lawful or unlawful in an extreme circumstance of self-defence, in which the very survival of a State would be at stake." The vote was tied 7-7 (one judge had died, reducing the number of judges to

14), but the proposition carried because of the president's tiebreaking power.

In effect, the Court delegitimized nuclear weapons as a war-fighting strategy but left open the question of use in "an extreme circumstance of self-defence."

This was just what the nuclear states needed to bolster their claim that nuclear weapons are only for defence. Accordingly, the advisory opinion did not alter their nuclear deterrence policies. The 200 pages of the judges' separate opinions put a sharper edge to the Court's presumed ambivalence. Three of the judges, Weeramantry of Sri Lanka, Koroma of Sierre Leone, and Shahabuddeen of Guyana, all of whom had voted no in the key vote, declared in their statements that the use or threat of use of nuclear weapons is illegal any time, any place. In other words, the passage was not strong enough for them. The seven who voted yes – Bedjaoui of Algeria, Ranjeva of Madagascar, Herczegh of Hungary, Shi of China, Fleischhauer of Germany, Vereshchetin of Russia and Ferrari Bravo of Italy – said that nuclear weapons would "generally" be contrary to the laws of war. These seven could not decide whether their use would be lawful in an extreme circumstance of self-defence in which the very survival of a state would be at stake. Four judges – Schwebel of the United States, Oda of Japan, Guillaume of France and Higgins of the United Kingdom – disagreed with both propositions and held that no general rule is possible, each case being decided on its own merits. Thus, a total of ten of the fourteen judges took the position either that nuclear weapons could never be lawfully used or that their use might be lawful only in the most exceptional of circumstances.

Taking the Law Toward Total Prohibition

Lost in the debate over what the numbers really added up to were two other votes in which the Court voted unanimously. In the first, the Court ruled that a threat or use of nuclear weapons should be compatible with humanitarian law and specific nuclear weapons treaties. In the second, the whole Court maintained:

> There exists an obligation to pursue in good faith and bring to a conclusion negotiations leading to nuclear disarmament in all its aspects under strict and effective international control.

Anticipating that the Court's inability to give a comprehensive condemnation to nuclear weapons would be perceived as acquiescing with the nuclear states to maintain the status quo, President Bedjaoui, in his separate statement, said that the fact that the Court was unable to go any further should not "in any way be interpreted as leaving the way open to the recognition of the lawfulness of the threat or use of nuclear weapons." He then gave a stinging indictment of nuclear weapons:

> The very nature of this blind weapon…has a destabilizing effect on humanitarian law which regulates discernment in the type of weapon used. Nuclear weapons, the ultimate evil, destabilize humanitarian law, which is the law of the lesser evil. The existence of nuclear weapons is therefore a challenge to the very existence of humanitarian law, not to mention their long-term effects of damage to the human environment, in respect to which the right to life can be exercised.

President Bedjaoui added that even if it uses a nuclear weapon only in defence of its very survival, a state cannot exonerate itself from compliance with the "intransgressible" norms of international and humanitarian law. It would be very rash to accord a higher priority to the survival of a state than to the survival of humanity itself.

Several judges abhorred the absence of a clear and comprehensive law on nuclear weapons. Judge Vereshchetin of

Russia said the Court cannot be blamed for indecisiveness in situations in which the law is itself inconclusive. Judge Guillaume of France held that, inasmuch as the law provides no definitive guidance, states remain free to act as they think fit in the exercise of their sovereignty. Contrary to Judge Bedjaoui, he maintained that, in recognizing the imperative of the survival of a state, the Court acknowledged the legality of policies of deterrence. Continuing this theme, Judge Fleischhauer of Germany said that a state could retaliate with nuclear weapons when attacked with nuclear, bacteriological or chemical weapons threatening its existence. But that was not the view of Judge Weeramantry. His 88-page dissent deals convincingly with every last argument advanced by the nuclear weapons states in support of their position, including deterrence, reprisals, internal wars, the doctrine of necessity, and the health hazards of all, including so-called mini nuclear weapons.

> My considered opinion is that the use or threat of use of nuclear weapons is illegal *in any circumstances whatsoever.* It violates the fundamental principles of international law, and represents the very negation of the humanitarian concerns which underline the structure of humanitarian law. It offends conventional law and, in particular, the Geneva Gas Protocol of 1925, and Article 23 (a) of The Hague Regulation of 1907. It contradicts the fundamental principles of the dignity and worth of the human person on which all law depends. It endangers the human environment in a manner which threatens the entirety of life on the planet.

While regretting that the Court did not hold that the use or threat of use of nuclear weapons is unlawful "in all circumstances without exception," Judge Weeramantry said that the Court's opinion does "take the law far on the road towards total prohibition." For his part, Judge Koroma of

Sierra Leone rejected outright the Court's contention that the current state of the law did not permit the Court to go further. The law exists in substantial and ample form to permit the Court to outlaw nuclear weapons. After analyzing the evidence, Judge Koroma came to the conclusion that nuclear weapons are unlawful in all circumstances:

> [Nuclear weapons] are incapable of distinguishing between civilians and military personnel, would result in the death of thousands if not millions of civilians, cause superfluous injury and unnecessary suffering to survivors, affect future generations, damage hospitals and contaminate the natural environment, food and drinking water, with radioactivity, thereby depriving survivors of the means of survival contrary to the Geneva Conventions of 1949 and the 1977 Additional Protocol I thereto.

A Legal Basis for Political Action

The effect of the World Court's advisory opinion was to provide, for the first time, a legal basis for political action to ban nuclear weapons.

Initially, the effect might seem minimal because the nuclear states are ignoring it, NATO is hostile to it and the media have generally marginalized it. But the opinion is a watershed because it made a strong statement of the law governing the threat or use of nuclear weapons: it effectively delegitimized nuclear deterrence. At the very least, nuclear proponents can no longer claim that nuclear weapons are a legitimate tool of warfare. The Court forcefully identified the elimination of nuclear weapons as the true solution to the risk of planetary catastrophe posed by the existence of nuclear weapons.

It is the highest-level legal push ever given to governments to get on with nuclear disarmament. It goes beyond the NPT's Article VI, which obliges nations merely to *pursue* negotiations on nuclear disarmament: the Court has deemed that such negotiations must be *concluded*. Moreover, it explicitly separated the two themes in Article VI: nuclear disarmament and general and complete disarmament. No longer can the nuclear powers credibly state that nuclear disarmament can only come in the context of general disarmament. The "ultimate evil" must be eliminated urgently.

By emphasizing that nuclear weapons are not exempt from the rules of humanitarian law, the Court, even though it was divided on the application of certain questions of law, brought the issue of nuclear weapons into the legal arena. It threw a spotlight on the laws of humanity and the dictates of the public conscience.

Judge Weeramantry, who started the Weeramantry International Centre for Peace Education and Research in Sri Lanka after leaving the Court, maintains his ardent stance on the illegality of nuclear weapons. In 2003, he told a seminar in Colombo:

> Nuclear weapons are illegal under international law because the usages established among civilized peoples, the laws of humanity and the dictates of the public conscience of the global community of human beings would all undeniably unite in condemning this monstrosity which can obliterate entire cities, destroy the environment and even extinguish all the culture and civilization built up by centuries of human efforts in one fell stroke. Can there be any doubt that all civilization, all humanitarian sentiment, all dictates of this public conscience would reject out of hand even the semblance of a contention that such a weapon could be brought within the bound of legality?

Interpreting the law on this matter is a complex process when one takes the view that any means of self-defence is valid. The nuclear proponents have, of course, taken this route. The search for security through technology led to the nuclear arms race, and the public – everywhere – was told this was necessary for self-defence. Our common humanity was denied, as if the moral problems of the obliteration of huge sections of humanity could be swept aside by technology. In secular culture, the maintenance of nuclear weapons has been rationalized away. No law expressly forbids the threat or use of nuclear weapons; the absence of such a law enables the nuclear proponents to drive onward. The World Court felt that it by itself could not *invent*, so to speak, a new law, but it clearly pointed the way to the political development of such a law, which would be built on a common understanding that humanitarian law does not permit mass killing.

The United States government, perhaps foreseeing the development of public opinion and future laws prohibiting the use of strategic nuclear weapons, has renewed its attention to the development of low-yield nuclear weapons. The "bunker-buster" is an example. It is claimed that the military target, not the surrounding civilian areas, would be struck, and thus the proportionality requirement of humanitarian law would be respected. This assumes that nuclear weapons can be *controllable*. I use the word in two senses: controllable in terms of the amount of radiation released, and controllable in that any use of a low-yield nuclear weapon would not escalate into major nuclear conflict. Thus the U.S. implies that nuclear weapons, when small enough, are not inherently indiscriminate. This gets into risk analysis, a subject the military planners delight in because they can soon develop all sorts of computer projections.

Low-yield nuclear weapons take us into a semantic legal game. How many people can be killed by a low-yield nuclear weapon before the killing is labelled indiscriminate? How far must the radiation spread before it is unacceptable? What is the physical or geographic measurement of damage before the law of proportionality is broken? No, all this is legal sophistry. The effects of heat, energy and radiation of a nuclear weapon, no matter its size, contravene every aspect of humanitarian law. The argument that collateral damage is not intended is the most disingenuous of all. As Judge Weeramantry points out, the perpetrator of a nuclear act cannot avoid legal responsibility for the consequences any less than a driver careering in a car at 100 km per hour through a crowded market street can avoid responsibility for the resulting deaths on the grounds that he or she did not intend to kill the people who died.

Humanitarian law must be applied to every use of every nuclear weapon. A return to humanitarian law, not technological refinements of the act of killing, is required for society to deal with the illegality of nuclear weapons. A nuclear weapons convention, prohibiting the production as well as use of all nuclear weapons in all circumstances is urgently needed. Lawmakers – i.e., politicians and government bureaucrats – must be awakened by public demand to pass such legislation. An ironclad law prohibiting all nuclear weapons must be made. This will happen only when the evil nature of nuclear weapons is recognized rather than denied, as it is today. By emphasizing our humanity, not our technological prowess, we can achieve a universal law criminalizing the production and use of all nuclear weapons.

PART IV

---

*Reviving Hope for a
Nuclear Weapons–Free World*

11

From Risk to Reason

Like a beautiful rose suddenly spotted in the middle of a thorny bush, a working paper appeared at the 2005 Non-Proliferation Treaty (NPT) Review Conference that sparkled amid the dull grey documents piling up. Known as *Conference Working Paper 41*, it outlined a path to a nuclear weapons–free world. Sponsored by Malaysia and Costa Rica, it offered an unusual combination of reason and hope.

The abolition of nuclear weapons cannot occur while states maintain security doctrines that rely on nuclear weapons. How can the rest of the world encourage them to change their course? This is a long-term job. Meanwhile, the urgency of stopping the proliferation of nuclear weapons calls for immediate action. How can these two conflicting themes be meshed into a single coherent strategy? This is the challenge taken up by two states that have risen above the diplomatic deadlock. Malaysia, a country of 23 million people on the South China Sea, is currently the leader of the Non-Aligned Movement. Costa Rica, with 4.1 million people, is often regarded as Central America's jewel for its enlightened approach to conservation. As well, Costa Rica gave up its army in 1948.

Their joint paper sensibly reflects an understanding that key legal, political and technical issues need to be addressed to provide confidence to the nuclear weapons states to negotiate complete nuclear disarmament. Rather than waiting for such issues to be addressed in a contentious atmosphere, the paper calls on states to identify these issues and develop them into viable policies. This is both a pragmatic and up-lifting approach.

The Malaysia–Costa Rica paper considers the step-by-step approach to nuclear disarmament too limiting because it has not brought the world much closer to the final goal of nuclear disarmament than when the NPT was adopted in 1970. Neither does a comprehensive approach offer much possibility for success because it is so strongly opposed by the nuclear weapons states. But an incremental-comprehensive approach – incorporating step-by-step measures within a comprehensive framework – offers the best route to the final destination. Thus, the paper builds on the Thirteen Steps agreed to in 2000 for systematic and progressive im-plementation of Article VI of the NPT, but places these in a comprehensive framework for complete nuclear abolition. By exploring legal, technical and political elements required for a nuclear weapons–free world, a work program can be developed focusing on the following:

- non-discriminatory general obligations, applicable to states and non-state actors, prohibiting the acquisition, development, testing, production, stockpiling, transfer, use and threat of use of nuclear weapons;
- interim control, protection and accounting of nuclear weapons and fissile material holdings;
- phases and steps for the systematic and progressive destruction of all nuclear warheads and their delivery vehicles;
- mechanisms for verifying the destruction of all nuclear weapons;
- mechanisms for ensuring compliance;

• an international organization to coordinate verification, implementation and enforcement under strict and effective international control; and

• disarmament and non-proliferation education to ensure that key sectors of society understand the importance of achieving and maintaining a nuclear weapons–free world and how they can contribute to this goal.

The paper approaches these issues in a problem-solving mode – calling for exploration of ways to address the security concerns of states – rather than a prescriptive or confrontational mode. Consideration of the elements required for the complete elimination of nuclear weapons would close gaps in knowledge and build confidence that the end goal could be reached. Next steps would come into view: diminishing the role of nuclear weapons in security doctrines, achieving a balance between transparency and protection of sensitive information, defining the role of societal verification, building individual responsibility and protection into the disarmament process while respecting state sovereignty, dealing with delivery systems and dual-use materials, particularly plutonium and highly enriched uranium. A number of economic and environmental issues could also be addressed, including possible financial assistance for disarmament and harmonizing environmental standards for destroying systems and disposing of fissile materials.

The paper argues that the best way to approach these issues is to follow a dual track consisting of both informational work to further explore the elements required for a nuclear weapons–free world and the start of negotiations leading to the conclusion of a nuclear weapons convention or a framework of instruments for the abolition of nuclear weapons.

The Route to a Nuclear Weapons Convention

A nuclear weapons convention (NWC) would be an international treaty achieved through negotiations that would prohibit the development, testing, production, stockpiling, transfer, use and threat of use of nuclear weapons, and would provide a framework for the elimination of existing arsenals. But it would be more than just a treaty: it would be an affirmation and implementation of customary law prohibiting weapons of mass destruction and an expression of the universal societal condemnation of nuclear weapons. The convention would include procedures for verifying compliance, dispute resolution and enforcement. By focusing on the complete abolition and elimination of nuclear weapons, a convention would enact a universal and non-discriminatory norm, enhancing both national security and international co-operative security.

Such a convention is precisely what Hiroshima mayor Tadatoshi Akiba and the organization Mayors for Peace see as the rational and achievable way out of the current nuclear quagmire, as we saw in Chapter 1. A wide range of civil society organizations share this view, particularly in light of their frustrations with the failed 2005 NPT Review Conference. The global spotlight is now shifting to ways to make progress towards a nuclear weapons convention, not as a replacement for, or in competition with, the NPT, but as a way to implement Article VI and thus ensure the viability of the NPT. The Malaysia-Costa Rica paper, in opening up the elements underlying a nuclear weapons convention before such negotiations would actually start, contributes to changing the present climate from gloom to hope.

Such a convention already exists in model form. An international consortium of lawyers, scientists and disarmament experts drafted it, setting out the legal, political and technical issues that need to be addressed. Costa Rica submitted the model to the U.N. General Assembly in 1997.

There it has languished, despite efforts by leading NGOs to put a spotlight on it. The nuclear weapons states pretend it does not exist, and the non-nuclear states have been focusing their attention on a small number of what they deem practical steps.

The current impasse underlines the reason why the model NWC should be re-examined. Its moment has come – in the sense of governments, NGOs, and the media taking it seriously and doing the spade work to illuminate its elements, which is exactly what the Malaysia–Costa Rica paper proposes.

The elements of the model NWC make a comprehensive package. They include the following:

- general obligations of states and individuals under a nuclear weapons abolition regime;
- a phased program for dismantling and destroying existing nuclear stockpiles;
- control mechanisms for nuclear facilities and materials;
- a verification regime;
- criminal liability for violators;
- protection measures for whistleblowers;
- dispute resolution and enforcement procedures;
- measures for dealing with delivery vehicles and dual use materials;
- national implementation measures;
- an agency for overseeing the convention;
- entry-into-force options;
- relationships to other nuclear-related agreements and regimes; and
- a protocol concerning nuclear energy.

As a group, these elements are not easy to deal with. Unless they are broken down and examined in concrete ways, it is too easy to dismiss the model convention as unachievable.

The first requirement is to muster the will to do serious work, and that may be the unforeseen consequence of the 2005 failure. Political will may be generated in like-minded states determined to find a way to make progress on the elimination of the worst of the weapons of mass destruction. The international community has already banned the use, threat and production of chemical and biological weapons in the Chemical Weapons Convention and the Biological Weapons Convention, but a complete ban on nuclear weapons does not exist. True, the NPT seeks to eliminate nuclear weapons, but the inclusion of both nuclear elimination and general and complete disarmament in Article VI has long given the nuclear powers a way to dodge their primary responsibility. Not even the International Court of Justice, which did separate the two elements of Article VI and said that states have an obligation to conclude negotiations for nuclear disarmament, has been able to move the nuclear weapons states from their stubbornness.

Why then could deliberations now on a nuclear weapons convention achieve what the NPT has been unable to? The first answer is that they may not be able to. The more thoughtful answer is that such a convention might well be the culmination of the international community discussing, in a good atmosphere, all the elements that underlie a new security regime that does not rely on nuclear weapons. The present atmosphere surrounding the NPT puts the nuclear weapons states and the non-nuclear weapons states at loggerheads. The rhetoric for nuclear disarmament, on the one hand, and non-proliferation, on the other, cancel each other out. States' allegiances are torn. The public is confused. The push for the ultimate goal of a nuclear weapons–free world is dissipated. And while confusion reigns, the threat of the actual use of a nuclear weapon grows.

Keeping the Goal in Sight

Drafting a nuclear weapons convention – the international banning of all nuclear weapons – concentrates the mind. It keeps the goal in sight while working on the steps. It would be a productive exercise, understandable by the public, whose support, indeed pressure, is so important.

Some will say that the exercise amounts to preaching to the converted, since the nuclear weapons states' obduracy is the fundamental problem and they will never sign a convention. Such a defeatist approach fails to recognize that considerable progress is possible despite the resistance of the nuclear weapons states and some of their allies. In fact, progress can be made in building political will, strengthening legal norms against nuclear weapons, planning the institutions to support a nuclear weapons–free world and taking steps to establish and implement some of the requirements.

The conjecture that all the nuclear weapons states would refuse to co-operate is certainly premature. China has a stated policy of support for a nuclear weapons convention, and its votes on disarmament resolutions at the U.N. show its willingness to move down this road. The United Kingdom has acknowledged that a framework of legal instruments would be necessary to fully implement the NPT. France and Russia can be expected to resist at first but might respond if the U.S. position shifts. India, which scorns the NPT as a discriminatory instrument, would be attracted by a non-discriminatory global ban on nuclear weapons. Movement by India would require Pakistan to move also, and here the position of China would be key. That leaves Israel and the U.S. Because of Israel's insistence that a nuclear weapons–free zone in the Middle East is conditional on a Middle East Peace settlement, one cannot predict what Israel would do. Because the country is so dependent on the U.S., the American position could be determinative.

The position of the U.S. on nuclear weapons stems from more than just the recalcitrance of the Bush administration. All administrations, going back to Truman's, have ensconced nuclear weapons in their national security policies and the security agreements they have made with allies. The U.S. nuclear umbrella is wide, covering not only the NATO countries, but also Japan and South Korea. The very fabric of U.S. diplomacy is woven around U.S. nuclear military might. The next president, whatever the 2008 presidential election brings, will not automatically dislodge U.S. military policy from its fixation on nuclear weapons. The U.S. can be expected to use its leverage on Russia, the U.K. and France not to move as well. Therefore, it is unrealistic to expect a U.S. signature on a nuclear weapons convention in the foreseeable future.

The Role of Middle-Power States

However, there are other factors are at work that a prospective nuclear weapons convention can tap into. Respected middle-power states, doing spade work and advocating for such a convention, are capable of influencing the nuclear weapons states. If the presidents and prime ministers of these countries show active leadership – which Kofi Annan is calling for – the chances improve. An international call could mesh with the advocacy of many civil society groups within the United States already working in a highly professional manner on nuclear disarmament issues.

The concerted effort to reach an understandable goal would raise world public opinion. In a new, more enlightened atmosphere, progressive steps may be possible that are considered unrealistic today.

Finally, suppose a nuclear weapons convention was negotiated among like-minded states but, in the end, the nuclear weapons states did not sign it. Would the effort be futile? Not at all. Such a convention, even without the requisite signatures, would raise the legal norm against nuclear weapons. It would enable world approbation to be directed at those states still brandishing their nuclear weapons despite a world ban. At the very least, this would force nuclear proponents to start explaining to their own publics why nuclear weapons are important while the rest of the world wants to get rid of them. These national debates are precisely what has been lacking in the nuclear weapons states where vested nuclear interests have either controlled or manipulated public opinion for too long.

The Ottawa Process, by which a group of like-minded states working closely with informed civil society groups produced an anti-personnel land mines treaty, may be a template for nuclear negotiations. The Ottawa Process started when the government of Canada (at that time the active Lloyd Axworthy was foreign minister) became disenchanted with the blockages at the Conference of Disarmament and simply called a conference of interested states to pursue a way to end the evil of landmines. The discussions led to negotiations on a treaty, which entered into force following the 40th ratification in 1998. It has now been signed by 153 countries. Some major states, such as the United States, Russia and India, have still not signed, but no one says the treaty is not worthwhile. It has led many countries to relinquish their landmines and moved the world community forward on a quest to ban landmines everywhere.

The idea that a nuclear weapons convention is a non-starter because the nuclear powers would oppose it needs to be re-examined. The Malaysia–Costa Rica paper opens the door to do so.

Any one of a number of countries or a combination of countries could start the process, just as Malaysia and Costa Rica took the initiative to write their paper. For example, a state that has already relinquished its nuclear weapons would have the credibility and moral stature to lead. Candidates here would be Argentina, Belarus, Brazil,

Kazakhstan, South Africa and Ukraine. The New Agenda Coalition (Brazil, Egypt, Ireland, Mexico, New Zealand, South Africa and Sweden) distinguished itself at the 2000 NPT Review Conference by negotiating with the nuclear weapons states to obtain the "unequivocal undertaking" for complete nuclear disarmament. It proved more difficult at the 2005 conference, with the focus on non-proliferation, for the Coalition to stay together; nonetheless, the fact that eight NATO states supported it at the 2004 U.N. General Assembly shows that it could lead to a new nuclear disarmament initiative.

Naturally, if a nuclear weapons state were to lead the process, the influence would be greater; such a possibility, while seemingly unlikely, should not be discounted. Also, a country belonging to NATO, with its rigid adherence to nuclear weapons, seems an unlikely candidate. Canada, Germany, Norway and Belgium all have good credentials, were it not for the NATO demand for institutional loyalty. Malaysia and Costa Rica, though well intentioned, likely do not have the weight to draw in Western countries. But they have already made a significant contribution though their paper, which does not ask for immediate negotiations for a nuclear weapons convention. Rather, they propose a new, open-ended process to examine the legal, political and technical requirement for a nuclear weapons–free world.

In this framework, without any pre-commitments to a nuclear weapons convention, it should be possible for a group of like-minded states deeply committed to Article VI of the NPT to begin working together on the legal, political and technical elements. Working together, initially without the nuclear weapons states present, would allow their creativity and commitment to surface. They would be concentrating not on the confrontational question of *whether* to abandon nuclear deterrence but on a collaborative exploration of *how* to replace the program of nuclear deterrence with one of abolition and alternative security mechanisms.

This work, in an Article VI forum, could specify steps to be taken unilaterally, bilaterally, regionally and multilaterally to enhance security, without relying on the nuclear weapons states. The work would be seen as a contribution to the NPT process. These like-minded states could come from the list of former nuclear weapons states, the New Agenda Coalition, NATO, the Non-Aligned Movement, leaders in the nuclear weapons–free zones, such as Mexico, and other key states, such as Japan. A champion among these potentially influential middle powers may yet emerge.

"Trust but Verify"

A nuclear weapons convention will only be effective when it can be verified in both political and technical terms. A guiding principle should be the search for a regime sufficiently restrictive to ensure the highest level of confidence in compliance, but also sufficiently permissive to allow states to join without jeopardizing their legitimate security interests and commercial activities.

The elimination of nuclear weapons requires a new architecture of security based on an adequate verification system. The components of a reliable verification system are coming into place, beginning with the inspection system maintained by the International Atomic Energy Agency and the monitoring systems maintained by the Comprehensive Test Ban Treaty Organization, which has the capacity to detect the most minute nuclear test explosions. On-site inspections of suspect materials will have to be part of the disarmament process (the U.S. and Russia pioneered this in the Intermediate Nuclear Forces Treaty of 1987).

The last of the Thirteen Steps deals with the verification required to ensure compliance with nuclear disarmament agreements. In the intervening years, the United Kingdom launched a study program to develop verification technologies and presented a working paper to the 2005 Review

Conference spelling out an approach to four key areas: authentication, dismantling, disposition and monitoring. The study concluded that many aspects of authentication of sensitive nuclear weapons designs are achievable. Using modern technologies, inspectors can safely dismantle nuclear warheads. Conventional safeguards systems can already handle the disposition of fissile material. Routine and challenge inspections can buttress a monitoring program. The working paper noted that "while considerable technology exists to support verification of a disarmament program, much still needs to be done in a number of areas to develop and prove these."

Trevor Findlay, a verification expert working in co-operation with the Verification, Training and Information Centre (VERTIC) has proposed a standing United Nations body to deal with verification of weapons of mass destruction. He presented his report, which was commissioned by the government of New Zealand, to the Commission on Weapons of Mass Destruction, whose own report is due in 2006. Findlay's study built on the experience of the U.N. Monitoring, Verification and Inspection Commission (UNMOVIC), which was mandated to deal with weapons of mass destruction in Iraq. Findlay presented a case that a standing body is both "necessary and feasible." He said: "Such a body would extend the range of tools and options available to the international community in tackling the threats of [weapons of mass destruction], including from non–State actors, as well as expand the frontiers of inspection, monitoring and verification."

Despite the importance the U.N. attaches to weapons of mass destruction, there is no single U.N. agency with a holistic, integrated view of the problem. For example, the International Atomic Energy Agency, which devotes itself to nuclear safety and security, does not concern itself with research, development and testing of actual nuclear warheads. The Comprehensive Test Ban Treaty Organization is equipped to verify testing but cannot ban preparations to test. The Biological Weapons Convention has absolutely no verification regime.

Building on the U.N.'s comprehensive approach to Iraq, a future U.N. verification body could:

- maintain a general watch on weapons of mass destruction and related developments worldwide;
- maintain generic data gathering, processing and analytical capacities for all types of weapons of mass destruction;
- keep abreast of developments and conduct training in verification modalities, techniques and technologies;
- maintain and develop a capability to undertake, at short notice, verification operations, including fact-finding missions, on-site inspections, ongoing monitoring and verification and complete verification operations, on request.

The Malaysia–Costa Rica paper also made a contribution to moving the subject of verification forward. It recommended the study of a number of possible mechanisms for verifying the destruction of all nuclear weapons, such as agreements among states on data sharing and stepping up monitoring activities through photography, radionuclide sampling and other data collection systems.

Obviously, international confidence must be built at each step, by showing that the new arrangements promote, not detract from, security. Verification establishes whether all parties are complying with their obligations under an agreement, and the success of any agreement depends on building an atmosphere of trust. This trust can only be maintained when all sides are aware that cheating is likely to be detected. Verification cannot provide 100 per cent certainty, but after several years of monitoring and inspection of chemical and biological weapons, and with the transition to low levels of nuclear weapons, a pattern of knowledge would be built up, so that confidence in the process would be high. If a non-nuclear weapons state tried to create a clandestine program to build nuclear weapons, the activities of reactors, even when underground, would be detected by remote infrared sensors. A properly financed and staffed verification agency, operating with the full co-operation of all the nuclear states, would make it unacceptably dangerous for any party to cheat on an agreement. If the verification provisions of an agreement are comprehensive, parties would be deterred from cheating because they know they run a high risk of getting caught. This is called "verification deterrence."

The possibility of "breakout" is another technical reason why the nuclear weapons states have refused to countenance complete nuclear disarmament. There is a concern that these states could cheat by retaining a secret cache of nuclear weapons or fissile material. While it is true that such a cache might escape external detection, no state contemplating cheating could be certain that its transgression would not be revealed from within. Any cheating would be known by a considerable number of citizens. While governments can legitimately require citizens to keep secrets relating to *lawful* national security concerns, they cannot require them to break international laws. If just one individual refused to go along with the deception and "blew the whistle," all would be revealed. A deviant government could never be sure that it would not be exposed from within. "Breakout" involves real risks of being caught and provoking international action against the offending state.

The potential for a state to break out of a nuclear weapons convention and pursue a nuclear weapons program will exist as long as nuclear material, including that produced by use of nuclear energy, exists. That is why international control of the nuclear fuel cycle, as discussed in Chapter 3, is essential. As progress is made in nuclear disarmament, and nuclear weapons themselves become stigmatized, the likelihood of a state successfully breaking out of a convention diminishes.

"Trust but verify," U.S. President Ronald Reagan famously said. Verification is essential, but the demand for a perfect verification regime is little more than an excuse for not seeking the elimination of nuclear weapons. Perfect security is not possible. Inevitably, some risk will have to be accepted if the wider benefits of a nuclear weapons–free world are to be realized. The rational approach is to evaluate comparative risks, not demand the elimination of risk. It is much more dangerous for the world to stay on its current course. Compared to the risks inherent in a world bristling with nuclear weapons, the risks associated with whatever threat a cheating state could assemble before it was exposed are far more acceptable.

Enforcement is another key element of a nuclear weapons convention. The drafters of the model convention felt that it would be more effective to persuade states to comply with the convention than it would be to have to respond to a violation with enforcement measures; however, the model does include provisions for enforcement, such as restricting states' rights, suspending assistance for nuclear activities, and other sanctions. Ultimate authority would remain with the U.N. Security Council. Since a threat or use of nuclear weapons constitutes a threat to the peace, Security Council action would be required.

The means to rid the world of nuclear weapons are at hand. Moral leadership and political will are now needed to implement those means.

12

Lifting up Our Eyes

Every effort must be made to conclude a nuclear weapons convention to ban the production and use of nuclear weapons, as I argued in the preceding chapter. Nuclear weapons must be formally declared illegal; any use anywhere for any reason must be codified as a crime against humanity. The deadlock in the operation of the Non-Proliferation Treaty combined with the increasing risk of the use of nuclear weapons, demand a focused effort to start building the architecture to support a nuclear weapons–free world. Time is urgent.

All this might be considered the short-term strategy. It cannot wait for the peaceful resolution of conflict around the world, as if regional tranquility must be achieved before the nuclear weapons states will give up their arsenals. Neither can we wait for humanity to overcome its proclivity for greed, as if a more compassionate human nature must emerge before society can lay down its instruments of mass destruction.

It is true that nuclear weapons are about far more than nuclear weapons. They are about power. They are about economic exploitation. They are about racism. They are about fear. Nuclear proponents have deceived the public for a long time that nuclear weapons are about deterrence, that they are necessary to ensure our own security and that their use, while regrettable, is justified to protect our way of life. Lies. Just as truth is the first casualty of war, the rationale constantly advanced for the possession of nuclear wars is deceitful and an insidious manipulation of public thinking.

A thorough analysis of the true reason for the continued existence of nuclear weapons leads into the terrain of the human psyche. The same is true of war. Is a war necessary to resolve a problem of aggression in any given circumstance, such as in Vietnam, Afghanistan or Iraq? Or is war the outcome of the determination of a political or military actor to defend vested interests? The military–industrial complex, a powerful influence in political decision making, benefits commercially from war and profits from the maintenance of the nuclear weapons systems. They do not want to let go, and seize on instabilities to make their case, always appealing to the fear, grief and anxiety of the human condition.

The human condition is clouded by aggression at the best of times. That may be expressing reality too mildly. We have fought wars throughout human history (though there have been intermittent periods of peace). The interaction of human beings always throws up conflict. And so the pessimists say that, human nature being what it is, we will always need to protect ourselves. We cannot expect angels to walk the streets of the world.

This view of humanity – dark, apprehensive, acquisitive – is a significant obstacle to a nuclear weapons–free world. Nuclear weapons have become part of the condition of continued existence in a decidedly imperfect world. Yes, they are dangerous, people tell pollsters. Yes, the world would be better without them. But behind a benevolent response lies lassitude borne of an interior conviction that the human condition is such that nuclear weapons will continue to exist. That is just the way it is.

The architecture for a nuclear weapons–free world – the strengthening of international law and verification systems – runs up against a primal need to change human thinking.

Human thinking does, of course, change. Legalized slavery, colonialism and apartheid were all done away with when societal thinking matured and people decided to develop the proper political and legal machinery. But such transformations take a long time.

How long will it take for the public mind to awaken, if not erupt, and decide that nuclear weapons are too dangerous a threat to the very development of the human condition that, through science, technology and the appreciation of human rights instruments, is making the world a better place? In other words, when will there be a public clamouring to excise the threat of nuclear weapons to the continuation of life on the planet?

Once such a clamour (call it a concerted campaign) starts up, and the public determines that it will be freed of the nuclear apocalypse, putting the pieces of the architecture for a nuclear weapons–free world into place will be much easier. The awakening of the public mind to the full benefits of life on earth without nuclear weapons is, perhaps, a long-term strategy. Human beings do not change overnight.

The short-term strategy needs the long-term strategy to be effective. The long-term strategy in turn needs the short-term strategy to give it focus and impetus. Both strategies need each other. They are interlocked. Immediate steps and a full vision are mutually complementary.

Is there vision to implement a two-pronged course of action? Governments, for the most part reeling with daily crises, cannot do this because the effects of the human condition have driven political leaders too far apart. Civil society, even that element most attuned to nuclear dangers, cannot take the lead because it does not have its hands on the levers of power. But players and groups within each can create a critical mass to move government machinery and public thinking forward. This fusion of effort occurred in the development of the anti-personnel land mines convention and the International Criminal Court, and it can occur in a growing movement to banish nuclear weapons from Earth.

It is not as if such an effort has to start from scratch. There is, in fact, considerable historical momentum behind the evolution of human rights thinking and the gradual tightening of the net on the moral and legal base for nuclear weapons. The strong legal basis of the Non-Proliferation Treaty as a result of the deliberations at the 1995 and 2000 review conferences, the advisory opinion of the International Court of Justice of 1996, the formation of the New Agenda Coalition, the discernible restlessness within NATO, the formation of the Abolition 2000 network, the growing effectiveness of research centres and other institutes, the public opinion polls: all of this constitutes movement forward. From an historical point of view, humanity has already begun the long journey from Hiroshima to a nuclear weapons–free world.

Of course, huge obstacles remain, in both the difficulties of creating an effective architecture and the pessimism of public thinking. It is these obstacles, reinforced by a media that focuses on the confrontational rather than the creative dimension of life, which we frequently dwell on. It is hard to work on both short-term and long-term actions when we feel so weighed down by, not to mention preoccupied with, the daily demands of ordinary life.

Still, recognizing the growing dangers to humanity and understanding that humanity truly is at a turning point in our long existence on the planet forces us to lift up our eyes. The very act of lifting up our eyes changes our attitude. And a changed attitude is the key to change.

So often when I give a lecture, people ask me, "What can I do?" The answer can vary, depending on one's circumstances. But a starting point for everyone – government official and civil society activist alike – is to lift up our eyes.

When we do, we will see the machinery already put into place through 60 years of United Nations activity. We see the legal instruments to protect human rights, the agencies and programs that provide development services and protect the environment, the treaties and agreements to curb the arms races. Why not put a nuclear weapons convention into place? Why not, indeed? Lifting up our eyes is the first step towards action.

Dialogue and Reconciliation

Looking beyond our immediate setting, we can see that exploring the legal, political and technical requirements for a nuclear weapons–free world is possible. This action, though focusing on the short term, involves the players in an exchange of views that breaks out of preconceived positions and opens up dialogue. Despite the endless talk at the United Nations, there is actually very little dialogue. This is because of the system of regional groupings.

When I was Canada's Ambassador for Disarmament from 1984 to 1989, I chaired weekly meetings of the Western ambassadors to plan strategy for disarmament talks. The East Europeans had their own group. So did the nations of the Non-Aligned Movement. Each group deliberated within its own framework. Then, frequently oblivious of what others were saying, each presented its own views. There was no intergroup exchange or cross-cultural dialogue to try to understand and respond to one another's views. The others were always seen as opponents rather than partners. Such myopia is particularly limiting in the field of security because all security is interdependent in the era of weapons of mass destruction: no nation or group of nations can achieve security alone. In recent years, a start at intergroup activity (the New Agenda Coalition is an example) has been made, but it is still primitive.

The oneness of humanity, an idea once considered the preserve of religion, is now a crass, pragmatic concern. In the modern world, we will live together or die together because nuclear weapons threaten to kill us all, so dialogue, to understand better all the implications of this unwanted unity, is now essential.

Dialogue, a sincere opening of the mind to the conditions and needs of others, is a firm step towards reconciliation. Reconciliation is at the heart of the long-range strategy. In my 2003 book *The Human Right to Peace*, I discussed how reconciliation is an integral feature of the culture of peace, and drew from the U.N.'s Dialogue Among Civilizations, from which UNESCO produced the book *Crossing the Divide*. Here I repeat that reconciliation is the highest form of dialogue. Reconciliation comprises the capacity to listen and the capacity not only to convince but also to be convinced and, most of all, the capacity to extend forgiveness. Reconciliation does not happen only at the institutional level; it is a challenge to the hearts and minds of individuals.

Reconciliation is a rejection of the limitations of the status quo. It requires confronting the truth. It demands that we first look into the eyes of peace – internal peace, peace with ourselves. Partnerships follow. This produces a global ethic for institutions and civil society built on a common longing for peace, justice, partnerships and truth.

There is no finer example of reconciliation in action today than the *hibakusha* of Hiroshima and Nagasaki. Hiroshima mayor Tadatoshi Akiba lauds them because they rejected hatred and revenge from the beginning. They do not see the human race as a collection of enemies. They refuse to view the human community as a tense standoff among selfish entities battling over territory and resources. Rather, they see all humans as members of one family, a single unit. Having experienced the ultimate consequence of animosity, the *hibakusha* deliberately envisioned a world beyond war in which the human family learns to co-operate.

When they tell their stories, one of the most common phrases they use is, "I do not want anyone else to suffer the way I did." They mean no one, not one single person. They have captured the truth of reconciliation. In opting for life in excruciating circumstances under which no one could have blamed them had they chosen death, they continue to teach us a lesson, Akiba says. "If we hope to survive the 21st century, we must emphasize that understanding the experience of the A-bomb survivors is among the most important tasks we face."

Reconciliation cannot be taught or imposed, though more dedicated education on disarmament requirements would be helpful. Neither is reconciliation a technique. It is essentially an attitude – a reaching out from within to contribute to a common elevation of human conduct. Though idealistic, it is achievable. Charismatic leaders such as Mahatma Gandhi and Martin Luther King practised it. It is certainly dangerous; charismatic leaders have been assassinated because they tried to cross the divide. Reconciliation is not for the weak of heart.

Active work for nuclear disarmament is a direct contribution to reconciliation, the full bloom of which may be a long way off. But we cannot wait for human reconciliation and the consequent relaxation of tensions around the world to develop a nuclear weapons convention. Urgency for survival and vision for human improvement have intersected.

13

Civil Society: Creative Ideas

When the Non-Proliferation Treaty (NPT) was indefinitely extended in 1995, the President of the Review Conference, Ambassador Jayantha Dhanapala of Sri Lanka, went to the podium for his closing speech. It was past midnight and the delegates were exhausted from the month-long meeting. After saluting the accomplishments of the conference's "truly unique encounter with history," Dhanapala turned his attention to the representatives from the non-governmental organizations (NGOs) in the galleries; 36 groups had made presentations at a noon-hour event held a couple of weeks earlier. Henceforth, he said, the expertise and resources of non-governmental organizations should be "integrated" into NPT meetings through written and oral presentations to "encourage the maximum exchange of ideas" between NGOs and delegates.

The role of civil society* in nuclear disarmament issues is long-standing, with many ups and downs in terms

---

* The term "civil society" is sometimes confused with "NGOs" (non-governmental organizations), a more familiar designation of people who, for the most part, volunteer their service to an organization with a cause. "Civil society" is a much broader designation, with a long list of actors, including academic institutions, business forums, consumer advocates, development co-operation initiatives, environmental movements, ethnic lobbies, faith-based of effectiveness. For the most part, civil society has taken a confrontational stance, with peace activists protesting against nuclear weapons and warning governments about impending disasters if they did not at least freeze nuclear development should they not "ban the bomb" entirely. Governments have customarily shown their disdain for the importuning of civil society, countering that NGOs did not know enough about the issues or, as was claimed during the Cold War, served as unwitting "commie dupes."

Despite government attempts to shunt aside the views of nuclear activists, public pressure is responsible for many of the gains that have been made in curbing nuclear weapons. This is a point Lawrence S. Wittner, professor of history at the State University of New York, Albany, emphatically makes in his scholarly trilogy, *The Struggle Against the Bomb*. His final volume, *Towards Nuclear Abolition: A History of the World Nuclear Disarmament Movement* (Stanford University Press, 2003), described how the Nuclear Freeze campaign in the United States, the European Nuclear Disarmament campaign and comparable movements around the world forced government officials to move towards nuclear arms control and disarmament. During the 1980s, when the Cold War peaked and the deployment of nuclear weapons exceeded 65,000, an educated, middle-class movement became a force to be reckoned with. Wittner wrote:

> At an exceptionally dangerous juncture in modern history, when numerous governments scrambled to build nuclear weapons and threatened to employ them for purposes of annihilation, concerned citizens played a central role in curbing the nuclear arms race and preventing nuclear war.

associations, human rights activists, labour unions, local community groups, peace movements, philanthropic foundations, professional bodies, relief organizations, think tanks, women's networks and youth associations. For more on this subject, see my earlier work, The Human Right to Peace (Novalis, 2003), ch. 9, "Civil Society: New Demands for a Humane World."

While a small group of government leaders – among them Olof Palme of Sweden, Andreas Papandreou of Greece, Rajiv Gandhi of India, and Mikhail Gorbachev of the Soviet Union – already shared the perspectives of the peace movement, most politicians and leaders viewed the nuclear disarmament campaign negatively because it challenged their reliance on nuclear weapons for national security. When NATO's deployment of Cruise and Pershing missiles in Europe went ahead in 1982, a wave of popular resistance had a political effect, even if it did not stop the deployment. The Six-Nation Peace Initiative (Argentina, Greece, India, Mexico, Sweden, Tanzania) of the 1980s was driven by Parliamentarians for Global Action, which was in turn organized by civil society leaders. Within a relatively short time, both the U.S. and the Soviet Union had replaced plans to build, deploy and use nuclear weapons with policies of nuclear restraint. A series of summits between presidents Gorbachev and Reagan, and later between Boris Yeltsin and George H. W. Bush, produced a number of disarmament agreements, which slowed down, then ended for the moment, the nuclear arms race.

U.S. officials have steadily claimed that disarmament gains were only possible because the U.S. achieved military superiority with "peace through strength" policies. Russian leaders, denying this, have stated that disarmament progress was made because of new thinking, which citizen activism had helped promulgate. Wittner points out that most government leaders find it embarrassing to admit that they were pushed into action, "for it reveals them not as steely-eyed, self-confident shapers of national destiny, but as beleaguered, apprehensive officials, giving way to the demands of a restive public. This is not their preferred image of themselves."

It was, in fact, the success of the anti-nuclear movement in the 1980s that led to its diminishment in the 1990s. This seems paradoxical, but as Wittner states, when the nuclear menace has been grave, the nuclear disarmament movement has been powerful; but in times of reduced danger, the movement has declined. In other words, when the Cold War ended as a result of social restiveness and protests, and nuclear weapons reductions took place, many people thought the nuclear crisis had been substantially eased, if not extinguished. They turned their attention to other threats to human security, such as issues related to sustainable development. As the 1990s came to a close, it was frequently remarked that the "steam" had gone out of the nuclear disarmament movement. When the NPT was indefinitely extended in 1995, the International Court of Justice gave its advisory opinion in 1996, and the Comprehensive Nuclear Test Ban Treaty was opened for signature that same year, it seemed that nuclear weapons problems were taking care of themselves. Nuclear testing by France, India and Pakistan did arouse some protests, but generally the public went to sleep on the nuclear issues.

In this benign climate, the Bush administration issued its Nuclear Posture Review, affirming nuclear weapons were here to stay and threatening new uses. The other nuclear weapons states continued their modernization programs. North Korea proclaimed itself the possessor of nuclear weapons; Iran was suspected of having them, too. The Second Nuclear Age began, but there was little public notice of it because public attention was riveted on the complex question of whether Iraq possessed weapons of mass destruction, the resultant war and the pervasive fears for security unleashed by the terrorist attacks of September 11, 2001.

In these disjointed times, many nuclear disarmament activists, unwilling to settle for anything less than a nuclear weapons–free world, have maintained an impressive record of work. Abolition 2000, a global network of 2000 organizations in 90 countries working to build the political will necessary for a global treaty to eliminate nuclear weapons, is a key group. It was created by the confluence of a number of streams.

In 1993, the International Peace Bureau (IPB), which won the Nobel Peace Prize in 1910, formed a coalition with three other international groups: the International Association of Lawyers Against Nuclear Arms (IALANA), the International Network of Engineers and Scientists (INES), and the International Physicians for the Prevention of Nuclear War (IPPNW)(winner of the 1985 Nobel Peace Prize). Its declaration, calling for a nuclear weapons–free world, was endorsed by 71 groups in 20 countries, augmented by affiliates in 100 nations. The World Campaign for the Abolition of Nuclear Weapons was set up by the Nuclear Age Peace Foundation of California. The World Court Project, launched by the IPB, IALANA and IPPNW, promoted the U.N. resolution that requested the advisory opinion of the International Court of Justice. The International Network of Engineers and Scientists Against Proliferation (INESAP) set up a working group of lawyers, scientists and others to draft a model nuclear weapons convention. Many groups, including Campaign for Nuclear Disarmament (Britain), Mouvement de la Paix (France), International Physicians for the Prevention of Nuclear War (Germany), Gensuikyo and Gensuikin (Japan), and Western States Legal Foundation (U.S.), worked with the European Test Ban Coalition to stimulate governments to negotiate the Comprehensive Nuclear Test Ban Treaty.

When key players from non-governmental organizations came to the 1995 NPT Review and Extension Conference, they pooled their strengths to lay the foundation for Abolition 2000: A Global Network for the Elimination of Nuclear Weapons. At first, the growing movement was split between those who favoured an indefinite extension of the NPT because it would lock in forever the obligations of the nuclear weapons states and those who wanted a 25-year extension because they feared the NPT would be weakened by the nuclear weapons states carrying on unchecked. The NPT was indefinitely extended, and Abolition 2000 called for the conclusion by 2000 of an international treaty requiring the phased elimination of nuclear weapons worldwide. When that deadline passed, the organizers, undaunted, started a new program, Abolition Now! The heavy turnout of NGOs at the 2005 NPT conference reflects Abolition 2000's growing strength. The organization is now working with Mayors for Peace.

These organizational developments have coincided with the exponential growth in the use of e-mail and the creation of websites on the Internet. New "communities of concern" are springing up electronically nearly every day. Despite the mainstream media's marginalization of the nuclear weapons crisis, civil society groups are highly informed.

Although a critical mass of the public has not yet been energized to pressure governments, the ongoing work of these groups gives lie to the claim by some that the peace movement is dead. If the quantity appears slight, the quality of work has never been higher. A brilliant example of this is Reaching Critical Will, a project of the Women's International League for Peace and Freedom, an organization dating back to 1915, when women in European countries then at war with one another met to protest the killing and destruction. Under the leadership of Jane Addams, who won the Nobel Peace Prize in 1931, the organization blossomed. When the U.N. started, the League stepped up its work to bring together women of different political views and philosophical and religious backgrounds to study and make known the causes of war and work for a permanent peace. In the past few years, Reaching Critical Will, led by Rhianna Tyson, has maintained a website; it collects, packages and often translates disarmament-related information into terms people can understand. More specialized information is provided by the Acronym Institute for Disarmament Diplomacy, headed by Rebecca Johnson, which publishes a journal containing analyses and strategic thinking on peace and security issues, with special emphasis on treaties and multilateral initiatives. The NGO Committee on Disarmament that functions at the U.N. has a long record of sponsoring panel discussions and publishes *Disarmament Times,* edited by Bhaskar Menon.

In the past decade, the work of civil society in the area of nuclear disarmament has been distinguished by growing interaction with governments rather than confrontation. A leading example of this is the Middle Powers Initiative, formed by eight international non-governmental organizations* specializing in nuclear disarmament. This group works primarily with middle-power governments to encourage and educate the nuclear weapons states to take immediate practical steps to reduce nuclear dangers and commence negotiations to eliminate nuclear weapons. (The Middle Powers Initiative defines middle-power countries as politically and economically significant, internationally respected countries that have renounced the nuclear arms race, a standing that gives them significant political credibility.) Since I am the Chairman of the group, it is perhaps more appropriate to draw from Professor Wittner's description:

> In December 1997, at the instigation of the Canadian Network to Abolish Nuclear Weapons, Douglas Roche, a Canadian senator and former disarmament ambassador to the U.N., began to form a network of leading international citizens' organizations, which came to be known as the Middle Powers Initiative (MPI). Drawing together [International Physicians for the Prevention of Nuclear War], [International Association of Lawyers Against Nuclear Arms], [International Network of Engineers and Scientists for Global Responsibility], the [International Peace

---

* Global Security Institute; International Association of Lawyers Against Nuclear Arms; International Network of Engineers and Scientists for Global Responsibility; International Peace Bureau; International Physicians for the Prevention of Nuclear War; Nuclear Age Peace Foundation; State of the World Forum; and Women's International League for Peace and Freedom.

Bureau], and other disarmament groups, the MPI sought to mobilize influential middle-power nations to commit themselves to immediate practical steps to reduce nuclear dangers – including a no-first-use policy and the de-alerting of nuclear forces – and to the abolition of nuclear weapons. When the New Agenda Coalition burst on the scene in June 1998, it had had no official contact with the MPI. But its program was virtually identical, and after Roche met with the officials in the Irish and Swedish foreign ministries, the two groups began a close relationship. This proved important, for the MPI, bolstered by groups like Abolition 2000, brought citizen pressure to bear upon governments around the world – particularly in NATO nations – that helped secure passage of the [New Agenda Coalition] resolutions at the United Nations.

Recommendations of the Middle Powers Initiative to the NPT

After its strategy consultation at The Carter Center in Atlanta, January 26–28, 2005, the Middle Powers Initiative made the following recommendation to the 2005 NPT Review Conference:

1. Balanced implementation of the NPT.
2. Reaffirmation of decisions made at 1995 and 2000 NPT Review Conferences.
3. U.S. and Russia to solidify and enlarge reductions under the Moscow Treaty.
4. Further reductions and elimination of tactical nuclear weapons.
5. U.S. and Russia to take their strategic weapons off alert status.
6. No new nuclear weapons; legally binding security assurances to be given by the nuclear weapons states.
7. Negotiations on a fissile material ban to be concluded; multilateral controls on uranium enrichment and plutonium reprocessing.
8. International Atomic Energy Agency's Additional Protocol to become universal standard.
9. Subsidiary body at the Conference on Disarmament to deal with nuclear disarmament.
10. Early entry-into-force of the Comprehensive Test Ban Treaty; present moratorium on testing to be maintained.
11. Deeper consideration of the legal, political and technical requirements for the elimination of nuclear weapons.

The Middle Powers Initiative, whose international steering committee includes former Canadian prime minister Kim Campbell, has sent many delegations to middle-power governments; the delegations have included Robert McNamara, former U.S. Secretary of Defense, General Lee Butler, former head of U.S. Strategic Command, and former U.S. ambassador Thomas Graham.

The Middle Powers Initiative has held many strategy consultations, notably at The Carter Center in Atlanta. In 2000, it brought together representatives of the New Agenda Coalition, NATO states and expert NGOs, along with six senior officials of the Clinton administration. Former President Jimmy Carter addressed the consultation. It contributed to the positive atmosphere at the subsequent NPT Review Conference, at which the "unequivocal undertaking" for nuclear disarmament was made. In 2005, President Carter invited the MPI to return for a repeat consultation to prepare policies for the 2005 NPT Review Conference. This time, 75 participants and observers attended, including high-level representatives of key governments and non-governmental expert practitioners. The consultation, which issued 11 practical recommendations, made the essential point that a balanced implementation of the nuclear disarmament and non-proliferation obligations of the NPT must be found; the bargain between the nuclear and non-nuclear signatories must be kept; a bridge among the centrist states, such as those of the New Agenda Coalition and like-minded NATO states, must be built to push a pragmatic agenda for the implementation of key priorities.

The MPI also works with parliamentarians and sponsors the Parliamentary Network for Nuclear Disarmament, which has 350 members in 61 countries. These parliamentarians receive non-partisan, up-to-date information on nuclear disarmament issues to help them formulate questions, motions and resolutions in their legislatures. The Global Security Institute, which houses the MPI operations, also runs the Bipartisan Security Group, which is dedicated to providing reliable information and analysis of global security issues to members of the U.S. Congress. The Global Security Institute, headed by Jonathan Granoff, focuses on strengthening international co-operation and security based on the rule of law. Its team includes former heads of state and government, diplomats, celebrities, religious leaders and Nobel laureates; the actors Michael Douglas and Pierce Brosnan and former supermodel Christie Brinkley have participated in Institute events.

MPI is not alone in interacting with governments. The Monterey Institute regularly holds workshops for government representatives at the Conference on Disarmament. The Simons Centre for Disarmament, part of the Liu Institute for the Study of Global Issues at the University of British Columbia, hosted a meeting of the government representatives on the Commission on Weapons of Mass Destruction, headed by Hans Blix. For several years, the government of Canada has conducted consultations with leading members of the nuclear disarmament community in Canada.

All this activity shows the growing maturation of the work of civil society in nuclear disarmament. It is buttressed by disarmament education programs, now growing in many countries. While Jayantha Dhanapala's call for the expert work of civil society to be "integrated" into the NPT process has not yet been fully realized, civil society is speaking out. However, the major governments do not appear to be listening. Their primary allegiance is to their own policies and alliances, not to the common good of humanity. Governments do not usually welcome sharing what has traditionally been their preserve. Many NGOs feel that they are not heard and that their participation has little impact on outcomes. For their part, governments frequently question the representivity, legitimacy, integrity and accountability of civil society groups. This tension may well continue to exist until a parliamentary assembly at the U.N. is some day elected to represent the will of the people of the world. This is certainly a long way off, but a number of current developments suggest that the voices of parliamentarians and civil society at the U.N. are getting stronger.

The Inter-Parliamentary Union, an international organization of 144 parliaments of sovereign states founded in 1889, is currently positioning itself to take on the role of a formal advisory body at the U.N. This may one day lead to a directly elected people's assembly at the U.N. Some kind of advisory, consultative or even decisive civil society assembly at the U.N. is talked about today to give flesh to the opening words of the U.N. Charter: "We the peoples of the United Nations...."

The Civil Society Millennium Assembly, convened by Kofi Annan in 2000, brought together more than 1,000 representatives of activist groups around the world, whom Annan dubbed "the Second Superpower." In 2005, the role of civil society took another step forward when consultations were held with key NGO figures on key elements for the 60th anniversary declaration: freedom from want, freedom from fear, freedom to live in dignity and strengthening the United Nations.

---

10 Things You Can Do For Nuclear Weapons Abolition

1. Stop and think for a moment about what the world would be like if 20 or more countries obtained nuclear weapons.
2. Join Abolition 2000 (www.abolitionnow.org).
3. Become a regional contact for the Abolition Now! Campaign.
4. Learn about the Model Nuclear Weapons Convention.
5. Discuss the nuclear weapons dangers with your family and friends.
6. Join a local group working on peace issues.
7. Organize and participate in a candlelight vigil at city hall on August 6 and 9 each year, calling for an end to the development and production of nuclear warheads.
8. Write to your legislators encouraging them to become active in nuclear disarmament issues.
9. Enroll your mayor in the Mayors for Peace Emergency Campaign to Ban Nuclear Weapons.
10. Believe that you can make a difference.

Throughout history, most great social movements, from the abolition of slavery to women's equality, have begun not with governments but with civil society. The integration of these pioneers into government processes was not, strictly speaking, essential. They built up public opinion for their causes and made governments respond. The measure of civil society's effectiveness is the results obtained.

A 2004 U.N. study of the role of civil society, headed by former Brazilian prime minister Henrique Cardoso, showed that effectiveness is growing. Previously, Cardoso said, governments would come together to discuss a new issue until there was sufficient consensus, which then led to government action. Today, it is more likely that civil society and a crescendo of public opinion bring an issue to global attention and that working coalitions of governments and civil society take the initial action. The development of the International Criminal Court is a case in point. Cardoso wants this work stepped up. His recommendation that the U.N. General Assembly enhance access to enable systematic engagement with civil society organizations was endorsed by the U.N. High Level Panel on Threats, Challenges and

Change, which said: "We believe that civil society and non-governmental organizations can provide valuable knowledge and perspectives on global issues." Kofi Annan followed this up by stating, in his respond to the High-Level Panel, that the U.N. should engage "much more actively" with civil society. "Indeed, the goals of the United Nations can only be achieved if civil society and governments are fully engaged."

In this current cycle of history, some people might think that minimal progress towards achieving the abolition of nuclear weapons has been made. Actually, as I have argued, there is a historical momentum for it. Though the obstacles in the way of abolition are gigantic, nuclear proponents are finding that they have less and less ground to stand on to justify retention.

The nature of the nuclear weapons problem — the very concept of human security — now requires a renewed two-pronged strategy by civil society: a push by abolition groups, constantly enlarging the critical mass of public opinion, augmented by the informed work of specialized groups integrating their ideas into government policies. Both approaches reinforce each other. The job of the Middle Powers Initiative and its counterparts is to show realistic ways to make progress; the job of Abolition 2000 and its partners is to build up the public demand for that progress. As more Western governments become disenchanted, even alarmed, at Washington's nuclear policies, the prospects of making an impact on governments go up. This is a time to move forward with creative, practical ideas, not succumb to Washington's will.

When a debacle like the 2005 NPT Review Conference occurs, it demoralizes many in civil society (not to mention the few dedicated government officials who have committed their personal work to progress in this area). Money for nuclear disarmament work is hard to raise. But those who truly understand the dimensions of the nuclear weapons threat must dive into their interior wellspring to restore the vision, energy and drive to find new and creative ways to challenge the political elitism that has caused so much discord and suffering. The continuing challenge to the status quo to make the culture of war give way to a culture of peace must be uppermost in our minds. A new spurt of activism by an enlightened civil society, fed by instant worldwide electronic communication, provides hope for change.

Conclusion

Destroying Five Myths

The campaign to eliminate nuclear weapons must dispose of five myths.

Myth #1: We must have regional peace first and then roll nuclear disarmament into general and complete disarmament.

The nuclear weapons states love this idea and promote it at every opportunity. It lets them off the hook for their legal obligations to act now to launch negotiations for nuclear disarmament. They try to pretend that, because Article VI of the Non-Proliferation Treaty (NPT) also talks about a treaty on general and complete disarmament, the two are inextricably linked: since the world is not moving to general and complete disarmament, they cannot do much to negotiate nuclear weapons elimination. The International Court of Justice has disposed of this myth by affirming that the priority of all nations must be to *conclude* negotiations to eliminate nuclear weapons. Nuclear weapons abolition is a prerequisite for peace. It is only when the world has moved away from the nuclear apocalypse that serious efforts can begin to reduce the levels of all weaponry and, most importantly, to reduce military spending for the sake of appropriating money to the needs of true human security.

Myth #2: We must abolish war first and then we can get rid of nuclear weapons.

This idea is promoted by some non–governmental organizations (NGOs) that consider that the main problem is
not the quality of the weapons as such but human proclivity
to war. Stamp out war, make it illegal for disputants to fight,
and then the nuclear weapons problem will take care of itself.
The elimination of war is certainly desirable and may one
day be achieved. After all, violence is not in the human genes
and, if future generations are socialized to shun war, maybe
humanity could take this giant leap forward. However, this
goal is too much to take on at this moment in history. The
architecture for a world without war needs to be developed,
and this will take a long time. Meanwhile, the urgency of
the nuclear weapons situation demands immediate action to
ensure the survival of the world now so that we can build
the machinery for permanent peace.

Myth #3: Nuclear weapons will always be with us because you can't put "the genie back in the bottle."

It is true that humanity will always have the knowledge
of how to build nuclear weapons, but that does not mean
that these weapons cannot be contained. A fence can be
built around that knowledge. The fence would consist of
international law. Though the knowledge of how to build
chemical and biological weapons is still with us, both these
classes of weapons of mass destruction have been outlawed.
If humanity does not outlaw nuclear weapons, it will be
sending a message to future generations that their presence
is tolerable.

Myth #4: You can't stop a nation from cheating, so a breakout from a nuclear weapons ban is always possible.

The advocates of this argument want the assurance of perfect security in the world. There is no such thing, and to suggest that we have to have it before eliminating nuclear weapons is an insult to our intelligence. What assurance do I have that I will not be shot dead on the street by a criminal? The chances of building an effective verification and compliance system to prevent a state from cheating and breaking out of a nuclear weapons ban go up in direct proportion to the determination of the international community to build such a system. The chances of a terrorist acquiring nuclear materials go down in direct proportion to the determination of the international community to put all nuclear fuels under multilateral control. The prospect of "whistle-blowers" – people who have direct knowledge that a state is preparing to build a nuclear weapon and report this knowledge to international authorities – should not be discounted. What is important here is for a global treaty banning all nuclear weapons, so that people everywhere know that it is against the laws of all nations to build nuclear weapons. Perhaps some risk will remain, but it will be far less than the risk we are running today by not insisting on a complete ban on nuclear weapons backed up with the force of international law.

Myth #5. Getting rid of nuclear weapons will make the world a perfect place.

This is a nice thought, but totally unrealistic and definitely not true. There will always be conflict in the world. It is not angels who walk the streets. But conflict can be resolved – it is the argument of this book that it must be resolved – without recourse to weapons that threaten the continuation of life on the planet. The elimination of nuclear weapons will not stop wars, end poverty, save the environment or guarantee the protection of all human rights. But without the political divisiveness, threats to use nuclear weapons and their enormous costs, the world has a better chance of successfully dealing with these other threats to security. The remaining weapons would be less threatening to humanity. The role of militarism would be reduced. A world in which wars were reduced to a minimum, and then contained, would be a big step forward for humanity.

★★★

These myths are at the core of the arguments of nuclear proponents that nuclear weapons are necessary for security, and they must be exposed for what they are – lies. The hypocrisy of the nuclear weapons states' argument that they themselves need nuclear weapons but no one else should have them must be challenged. It is not only the nuclear weapons states that are lying and endangering world security. All 23 non-nuclear members of NATO, who say that the Non-Proliferation Treaty is very important to them, are also guilty of fabricating the myths that they are truly adhering to their legal obligation to negotiate the elimination of nuclear weapons. In fact, they are not because they continue to endorse the U.S.-driven NATO policy that nuclear weapons are "essential."

Exposure of the myths, the growing maturation of nuclear disarmament work by the highly informed leaders of civil society, and the inherent dislike of nuclear weapons by the general public are gradually helping to lift up the prospects for action towards nuclear disarmament. One day, future generations will look back in disgust on a supposedly civilized society that accepted the absurdity of nuclear weapons as cherished government policy.

The abolition of nuclear weapons is no longer just a lofty goal, a noble aspiration, an idealistic thought. It has become the irreducible essential for survival. Peace is impossible as long as the threat of nuclear war hangs over our heads. Moving the world beyond the horrors of Hiroshima into a new frontier of human living must now claim our attention.

Chapter Notes

Chapter 1

The Spirit of Hiroshima, published by the Hiroshima Peace Memorial Museum, contains graphic descriptions of the effects of the bombing. The Mayors for Peace website (www.pcf.city.hiroshima.jp/mayors/english/) describes the Vision 2020 Campaign. *Hiroshima: In Memoriam and Today,* Hitoshi Takayama (ed.), published by the Himat Group, Japan, 2000, contains the stories of many of the survivors, along with a history of the city.

Chapter 2

Full reports and documents of the 2005 Review Conference of the Non-Proliferation Treaty (NPT) are found on the U.N.'s website (www.un.org/events/npt2005/) and the Reaching Critical Will website (www.reachingcriticalwill.org/), which is maintained by the Women's International League for Peace and Freedom. A further document, *Nuclear Disarmament: What Now?,* published by Reaching Critical Will, examines in detail what has and has not happened to the Thirteen Practical Steps of the 2000 NPT Review Conference. The same organization has produced a highly informative document, *The Model Nuclear Inventory* (Rhiana Tyson, editor), which tracks the military and civilian nuclear materials, weapons, locations and policies of each of the 44 states listed as having significant nuclear capabilities. A comprehensive presentation of NPT history and current issues is contained in *NPT Briefing Book*, published by the Mountbatten Centre for International Studies, University of Southampton, and the Center for Nonproliferation Studies, Monterey Institute of International Studies. Material depicting the nuclear weapons modernization programs of the nuclear weapons states is drawn from the NGO presentation to the NPT Conference by the Western States Legal Foundation (www.wslfweb.org) and the Lawyers' Committee on Nuclear Policy (www.lcnp.org). Basic sources are principally the Natural Resources Defense Council (www.nrdc.org), the *Bulletin of the Atomic Scientists* (www.thebulletin.org) and government documents. Of particular note is *War Is Peace, Arms Racing Is Disarmament: The Non-Proliferation Treaty and the U.S. Quest for Global Military Dominance*, (www.wslfweb.org/docs/warispeace.pdf), published by the Western States Legal Foundation, May 2005. Robert McNamara's article appeared in *Foreign Policy*, published by the Carnegie Endowment for International Peace, Washington, D.C., May–June, 2005. I attended the entire NPT Review Conference and subsequently wrote a political analysis, *Deadly Deadlock*, which is available on my website (www.douglasroche.ca/). I have drawn from this analysis in chapters 2 and 3. My earlier book on the 1995 NPT Review and Extension Conference, *An Unacceptable Risk: Nuclear Weapons in a Volatile World,* provides background on that event.

Chapter 3

An excellent analysis of the issues the NPT Review Conference faced is found in a series of briefing papers published by the British American Security Information Council and the Oxford Research Group. See www.basicint.org and www.oxfordresearchgroup.org.uk.

The report of the U.N. Secretary-General's High-Level Panel on *Threats, Challenges and Change, A More Secure World: Our Shared Responsibility* (www.un.org/secureworld) was published in 2004 and was responded to by Kofi Annan's document *In Larger Freedom:Towards Development, Security and Human Rights for All* (A/59/2005) (www.un.org/largerfreedom). Extensive material on the New Agenda Coalition is found on the website of the Middle Powers Initiative (www. middlepowers.org/), which held a forum January 26–28, 2005 at The Carter Center in Atlanta to flesh out the moderate elements for a successful NPT Review Conference first advanced by the New Agenda Coalition in its 2004 resolution at the General Assembly, *Accelerating the Implementation of Nuclear Disarmament Commitments* (www.middlepowers. org/mpi/archives/000237.shtml). Helpful material on issues related to the nuclear fuel cycle is contained in *Universal Compliance: A Strategy for Nuclear Security*, published by the Carnegie Endowment for International Peace,Washington, 2005 (www.carnegieendowment.org/publications); also *Multilateral Approaches to the Nuclear Fuel Cycle, the Expert Group Report to the Director General of the IAEA*, published by the International Atomic Energy Agency,Vienna, 2005 (www.iaea.org/Publications/Documents/Infcircs/2005/ infcirc640.pdf). NATO's nuclear policies in relation to the NPT are fully examined in Middle Powers Initiative briefing material. A detailed report of NATO's deployment of nuclear weapons is contained in *U.S. Nuclear Weapons in Europe* by Hans M. Kristensen, published by the Natural Resources Defense Council, February 2005 (www.nrdc. org/nuclear/euro/contents.asp). The latest rendition of NATO's unswerving position that its nuclear policies have "continued validity" is contained in the *Final Communique of the Ministerial Meeting of the Defence Planning Committee and the Nuclear Planning Group*, June 9, 2005 (www.nato.int/ docu/pr/2005/p05-075e.htm). A report of the special landmark conference of states belonging to nuclear weapons–free zones, including the declaration adopted, was presented by Mexico to the NPT Conference (NPT/Conf.2005/WP.46) (www.un.org/events/npt2005/working%20papers.html).

It includes the report of the Civil Society Forum, a side event, presented by Alyn Ware, Global Coordinator of the Parliamentary Network for Nuclear Disarmament. The only committee report on substantive issues to reach the NPT final plenary contained the working papers of the chairman of the subsidiary body on nuclear disarmament and security assurances. Even though it was stated that this material did not win consensus, it is valuable in pointing the way forward. See NPT/Conf.2005/MC.I/1 (www.un.org/events/npt2005/working%20papers.html).

Chapter 4

The testimony of Takashi Hiraoka, former Mayor of Hiroshima, is found in his deposition to the International Court of Justice, November 7, 1995 (http://www.pcf.city.hiroshima.jp/peacesite/indexE.html). As noted in the chapter, the Voice of Hibakusha (www.inicom.com/hibakusha) contains gripping accounts of the disaster. I have also reflected on the meaning of Hiroshima and Nagasaki in my earlier work, *The Ultimate Evil* (James Lorimer & Company, Toronto, 1997). There is a great amount of literature on Hiroshima and Nagasaki, starting with John Hersey's long article, "Hiroshima," published in *The New Yorker,* August 31, 1946, a year after World War II ended. The issue sold out within hours and a subsequent book (published by Alfred A. Knopf) was sent by the Book-of-the-Month Club free to all its members. An in-depth analysis of the lingering "Hiroshima problem" is found in *Hiroshima in America: Fifty Years of Denial,* by Robert Jay Lifton and Greg Mitchell (G.P. Putnam's Sons, New York, 1995).

Chapter 5

The effects of nuclear testing are dealt with in *No Immediate Danger: Prognosis for a Radioactive Earth*, by Rosalie Bertell (The Women's Press, London, 1985). See also "Health and Environmental Effects of the Production and Testing of Nuclear Weapons" (www.Nuclearfiles.org).

Many accounts of near-accidents with nuclear weapons are contained in *The Human Factor and the Risk of Nuclear War* (Claes Andreasson, ed.), a publication issued by the Swedish section of International Physicians for the Prevention of Nuclear War. The story of Colonel Stanislav Petrov has appeared in many publications and websites (among them www.brightstarsound.com/world_hero/article.html) and, most recently, Mark McDonald's article for Knight Ridder Newspapers, December 16, 2004 (www.vivelecanada. ca/article.php/20041219142655443). The TTAPS nuclear winter study was written about extensively by Carl Sagan and published by The School of Cooperative Individualism (www.cooperativeindividualism.org/sagan_nuclear_winter. html). The School's website contains excerpts from Carl Sagan's book *Cosmos* (www.cooperativeindividualism.org/ sagan_cosmos_who_speaks_for_earth.html). The TTAPS study was greeted by considerable controversy, especially from the political right, which found unacceptable the possibility that large-scale nuclear war might have disastrous environmental, economic and social consequences. The medical consequences of "bunker-busters" are examined by International Physicians for the Prevention of Nuclear War in its publication *The Threat of Low-Yield Earth-Penetrating Nuclear Weapons to Civilian Populations* (www.ippnw. org/NukeEPWs.html). The Union of Concerned Scientists has more to say on the subject (see www.ucsusa.org/global_security/nuclear_weapons/page.cfm?pageID=1170). The Canberra Commission report can be found at www. dfat.gov.au/cc/cc_report_exec.html. It provides a thorough rebuttal to all the political arguments advanced against the abolition of nuclear weapons.

Chapter 6

The Union of Concerned Scientists (www.ucsusa.org) and the Center for Defense Information (www.cdi.org) present helpful analyses of the problem of space weapons. For an excellent overview, see "Weapons in the Heavens: A Radical and Reckless Option," by Michael Krepon, President emeritus of the Henry L. Stimson Center, published in *Arms Control Today*, November 2004 (www.armscontrol.org/act/2004_11/Krepon.asp?print). General Lord's statement was in his Keynote Address to the National Space and Missile Materials Symposium, Seattle, June 22, 2004. An unusual but educative website is Howstuffworks (www.howstuffworks.com); an article on that site, "How Space Wars Will Work," by Kevin Bonson, explains the technologies now being developed to fight wars in space. The Pentagon's website (www.defenselink.mil) makes very clear U.S. intentions to achieve superiority in this new field. See the United States Joint Forces Command website (www.jfcom.mil/about/transform.html) for a clear declaration of space superiority. Jonathan Dean, Advisor on International Security Issues, Union of Concerned Scientists, offers a full explanation of the strengths and weaknesses of the Outer Space Treaty in *The Current Legal Regime Governing the Use of Outer Space.* (www.ploughshares.ca/content/ABOLISH%20NUCS/OuterSpaceConf02/DeanConf2002.html). His colleague, David Wright, Co-Director and Senior Scientist, Global Security Program, gave an informative presentation on key issues in the space weapons debate at a conference, "Safeguarding Space Security: Prevention of an Arms Race in Outer Space" (www.unidir.ch/pdf/activities/pdf-act269.pdf) held in Geneva in March 2005. Theresa Hitchens, Vice-President of the Center for Defense Information, presented a thorough analysis of U.S. policies at this event. The sponsorship of the conference is interesting: The People's Republic of China, the Russian Federation, the Simons Centre for

Disarmament and Non-Proliferation Research, Canada, and the United Nations Institute for Disarmament Research. Disarmament Diplomacy, published by the Acronym Institute, features material on the Russia-China draft treaty on space weapons (www.acronym.org.uk/dd/dd66/66nr07. htm). The case for a space weapons treaty is thoroughly made in *Common Security in Outer Space and International Law*, by Detlev Wolter, which I read in manuscript form.

Chapter 7

U.S. Senator Sam Nunn's address "The Race Between Cooperation and Catastrophe" (www.nti.orglc_press/ speech/nunnpressclub_030905.pdf) was given to the Conference on Nuclear Security convened by the International Atomic Energy Agency on March 16, 2005, in London. The Nuclear Threat Initiative, which Senator Nunn co-chairs, has an informative website (www.nti.org). Graham Allison's book *Nuclear Terrorism: The Ultimate Preventable Catastrophe* (Times Books, Henry Holt and Company, LLC, New York, 2004; www.nuclearterror.org) provides a comprehensive examination of the nuclear terrorist threat. Senator Nunn praises it: "For everyone from national security specialists trying to define a strategy to parents who want to leave their children a world worth living in, Graham Allison's book is essential reading." Nonetheless, because it ignores the necessity of the abolition of nuclear weapons, it is far from complete. Background reading is found in *Terrorism and the U.N.: Before and After September 11*, Jane Boulden and Thomas G. Weiss (eds.), Indiana University Press, 2004. A depiction of possible terrorist attacks ahead is given by Richard A. Clarke, National Coordinator for Security and Counter-Terrorism for presidents Bill Clinton and George W. Bush, in "America Attacked: The Sequel," *The Atlantic*, January–February, 2005. Time portrayed A.Q. Khan as "The Merchant of Menace" in its February 14, 2005, issue.

The Nuclear Control Institute (www.nci.org) is an excellent source for information explaining how even relatively small amounts of enriched uranium or plutonium could be used by terrorists to fashion a nuclear device. U.N. Security Council Resolution 1540 has been expertly analyzed by Alistair Millar and Morten Bremer Maerli in their paper "Nuclear Non-Proliferation and United Nations Security Council Resolution 1540," published in *Policy Briefs on the Implementation of the Treaty or the Non-Proliferation of Nuclear Weapons* by the Norwegian Institute of International Affairs (www.nupi.no/IPS/filestore/PolicyBriefsApril2005.pdf).

Chapter 8

Judge Christopher Weeramantry, a former judge on the International Court of Justice and now president of the International Association of Lawyers Against Nuclear Weapons, lives in Sri Lanka and experienced the effects of the tsunami first-hand. He wrote an editorial, "The Tsunami and Nuclear Weapons" (www.lcnp.org/pubs/IALANA2005/IALANAnews-02.htm). I wrote a column, "The Tsunami, God and a Nuclear Catastrophe," which appeared in the Edmonton Journal on January 3, 2005 (www.gsinstitute.org/pnnd/Tsunamigodandnuclearcatastrophe.htm). I have also drawn from "Tsunami Response: Lessons Learned" (http://tinyurl.com/8sjxl), testimony by Raymond C. Offenheiser, President, Oxfam America, to the U.S. Senate Foreign Relations Committee, February 10, 2005. The list of facts concerning the extent of poverty in the world and material on international aid response are on the website of the U.N. Millennium Project (www.unmillenniumproject.org/facts/index.html). *State of the World: Redefining Global Security 2005*, published by the World Watch Institute (W.W. Norton & Company, New York, 2005; www.worldwatch.org/pubs/sow/2005), provides an excellent analysis of the interplay between modern security issues. The opening essay,

"Redefining Security," by Michael Renner is particularly helpful. *The Annual Yearbook of the Stockholm International Peace Research Institute* is an excellent source of data on military spending. The specifics of U.S. spending on nuclear weapons are contained in *Atomic Audit*, Stephen Schwartz (ed.) Brookings Institution Press, 1998. The report on implementing the Millennium Development Goals by the team of economists headed by Jeffrey Sachs is entitled *Investing in Development* (www.unmillenniumproject.org/reports/index.html). His new book, *The End of Poverty: Economic Possibilities for Our Time* (Penguin Group, U.S.A., 2005), provides a blueprint for overcoming poverty. But like much literature on this subject, the link between poverty and high military spending is insufficiently addressed. U.N. Secretary-General Kofi Annan's report *In Larger Freedom: Towards Development, Security and Human Rights for All*, March 2005, is U.N. document A/59/2005 (www.un.org/largerfreedom). *It follows up the Report of the Secretary-General's High-Level Panel on Threats, Challenges and Change.*

Chapter 9

I first wrote about Sister Ardeth Platte in *Catholic New Times*, Toronto, January 16, 2005. A great deal of information about the non-violent resistance practised by her religious community is provided on the Jonah House website (www.jonahhouse.org).

A collection of statements on nuclear weapons by a variety of religious bodies and religious leaders is found in the website "Zero Nukes: A Project of the Interfaith Committee for Nuclear Disarmament" (www.zero-nukes.org/religiousstatements1.html). The moderator is Howard W. Hallman, Chair, Methodists United for Peace and Justice (hallman@zero-nukes.org). The website contains "A Moral Appeal for a Safer World Without Nuclear Weapons" (www.zero-nukes.org/moralappeal.html), which viewers can sign. The statement signed by 75 U.S. Catholic bishops condemning nuclear deterrence polices was prepared and published by Pax Christi (www.paxchristi.net), a Catholic peace organization operating in more than 30 countries. Pax Christi's work is based on the theme of a culture of peace, with reconciliation at the centre of its spirituality. It strives for dialogue with all NGOs – Christian, Muslim, Jewish, or non-religious – through conferences, seminars and fact-finding missions. The Russell-Einstein Manifesto is found on the website of Pugwash Conferences on Science and World Affairs (www.pugwash.org). The last living signer is Sir Joseph Rotblat, a scientist on the Manhattan Project who later renounced nuclear weapons. With Pugwash, he won the Nobel Peace Prize in 1995 for his work to abolish nuclear weapons.

Chapter 10

I have drawn principally on the advisory opinion of the International Court of Justice of July 8, 1996 (http://tinyurl. com/ahkn6), and especially the dissenting opinion of Judge Christopher Weeramantry, which is reproduced in *Nuclear Weapons Are Illegal: The Historic Opinion of the World Court and How It Will Be Enforced*, by Ann Fagan Ginger (ed.) (Apex Press, New York, 1998). This book carries the views of all the judges involved in the nuclear weapons case. In my earlier book, *The Ultimate Evil* (Lorimer, 1997), I analyzed the World Court's opinion and I have drawn particularly from pages 47 to 49 of that book for this work. I am grateful to the Lorimer company for this permission. The definitive work on the question may well be Judge Weeramantry's book *Nuclear Weapons and Scientific Responsibility,* first published by Sarvodaya Visha Lekha and Kluwer Law International, Sri Lanka, in 1987 and re-issued in 1999, following the World Court's advisory opinion. Judge Weeramantry has given an excellent summation of his views in "Illegality of Nuclear

Weapons," Proceedings of a Seminar, October 24, 2003, in Colombo, Sri Lanka, published by the Weeramantry International Centre for Peace Education and Research. The book *Nuclear Weapons and International Law in the Post Cold War World*, by Charles J. Moxley, Jr. (Austin & Winfield, Lanham, New York, Oxford, 2000), is a towering addition to the literature on this subject. Also very helpful is *The (Il)legality of Threat or Use of Nuclear Weapons: A Guide to the Historic Opinion of the International Court of Justice*, by John Burroughs (Transaction, 1998), sponsored by the International Association of Lawyers Against Nuclear Arms, one of the originators of the World Court Project, of which Burroughs was legal coordinator. An interesting background article is "The Nuclear Crucible: The Moral and International Law Implications of Weapons of Mass Destruction," by Terrence Edward Paupp, J.D., which discusses the modern divorce of moral constraint from nuclear technology (see www. nuclearfiles.org).

Chapter 11

The Malaysia–Costa Rica Working Paper, (NPT/ CONF.2005/WP.41), (www.un.org/events/npt2005/ working%20papers.html), is entitled *Follow-up to the Advisory Opinion of the International Court of Justice on the Legality of the Threat or Use of Nuclear Weapons: Legal, Technical and Political Elements Required for the Establishment and Maintenance of a Nuclear Weapon–Free World*. The Model Nuclear Weapons Convention is U.N. document A/C.1/52/7. The organizations principally responsible for drafting it were the International Association of Lawyers Against Nuclear Arms, International Network of Engineers and Scientists Against Proliferation, and International Physicians for the Prevention of Nuclear War. An excellent analysis as well as commentaries are contained in *Security and Survival: The Case for a Nuclear Weapons Convention*, published by IPPNW,

Cambridge, Massachusetts. The principal authors were Merav Datan and Alyn Ware. A Working Paper, *Snaring the Sun: Opportunities to Prevent Nuclear Weapons Proliferation and Advance Nuclear Disarmament Through an Abolition Framework*, by Alyn Ware, Kate Dewes and Michael Powles, is available at Peace Foundation Disarmament and Security Centre (www.disarmsecure.org). It shows how nuclear abolition, once a utopian ideal, has now become a political possibility that must be grasped and implemented. (Maori legend has it that the sun once raced across the sky making the days too short. Mauri and his brothers used flax ropes to snare the sun and slow it down for the benefit of all humanity. Can the proliferation of nuclear weapons – mini-suns themselves – be similarly constrained and the abolition of nuclear weapons achieved for the security of all humanity?)

Chapter 12

Crossing the Divide: Dialogue Among Civilizations (South Orange, NJ: Seton Hall University, 2001), which emerged out of dialogues UNESCO sponsored as a contribution to the International Decade for a Culture of Peace, contains profound insights into the concept and practice of reconciliation.

Chapter 13

Professor Lawrence S. Wittner's book *Toward Nuclear Abolition: A History of the World Nuclear Disarmament Movement* (Stanford University Press, California, 2003) is the third volume of his trilogy, *The Struggle Against the Bomb.* It is extensively researched and highly recommended. I am grateful to Colin Archer for permission to draw on his article, "The Creation of the Abolition 2000 Network," which was published in *Information Bulletin* (April 2005) by the International Network of Engineers and Scientists Against Proliferation. The Abolition Now! website (www.

abolitionnow.org) contains stimulating material to help anyone interested in becoming involved in nuclear disarmament
work. Similarly, the websites of the Middle Powers Initiative
(www.middlepowers.org) and the Global Security Institute
(www.gsinstitute.org) provide background information on
the work of both organizations. The report of the Middle
Power Initiative's 2005 consultation on the future of the
NPT is contained in *Nuclear Disarmament and Non-Proliferation: A Balanced Approach. The Cardoso Report of the Panel of
Eminent Persons on United Nations* – Civil Society Relations
is U.N. document A/58/817.

Nuclear Disarmament Websites

*There are many websites dealing with nuclear disarmament.
The following were helpful in preparing this book. Each contains
valuable perspectives on the nuclear disarmament agenda.*

Abolition 2000

www.abolition2000.org

Abolition 2000 is a network of more than 2,000 organizations committed to working for a nuclear weapons–free
world. The network has launched its own campaign called
Abolition Now! to build the political will necessary for
national governments to come together to negotiate the
dismantling of all nuclear weapons. Its secretariat is located at
the Polaris Institute in Ottawa. The Abolition 2000 website
is an excellent place to start for those wanting to familiarize
themselves with the global push for nuclear disarmament.

Acronym Institute for Disarmament Diplomacy

www.acronym.org.uk

Since 1997, the Acronym Institute for Disarmament
Diplomacy has published Disarmament Diplomacy, a
journal covering topics such as disarmament negotiations,
multilateral arms control and international security. The
journal is available free online. In addition, the Institute also
features a list of states known to possess weapons of mass
destruction.

Arms Control Association

www.armscontrol.org

The Arms Control Association is a U.S. non-partisan membership organization dedicated to furthering a better understanding of arms control policies. Its flagship publication is *Arms Control Today,* which is aimed at policy-makers, media and laypeople and features analyses of topics such as arms control, negotiations and agreements. The publication is available online free of charge.

British American Security Information Council

www.basicint.org

The British American Security Information Council (BASIC), a progressive, independent advocacy and analysis organization, focuses on armament and disarmament, global security and nuclear policy formation. BASIC provides occasional papers on international security policy in addition to nuclear, weapons of mass destruction and other weapons trading.

Canadian Network to Abolish Nuclear Weapons

www.web.net/~cnanw

The Canadian Network to Abolish Nuclear Weapons (CNANW) was established in 1996 by representatives of national organizations that believe that nuclear weapons are immoral and should be abolished. The network provides educational resources, such as videos, presentations, handouts and posters.

Canadian Pugwash Group

www.pugwashgroup.ca

The Canadian arm of Pugwash International issues periodical updates on nuclear disarmament issues in the form of statements, policy papers, interviews and articles. The group comprises Canadian experts on nuclear disarmament, conflict resolution and global security as well as environmental, social and health issues.

Carnegie Endowment for International Peace

www.carnegieendowment.org

The Carnegie Endowment for International Peace gathers together leading experts on international affairs, many of whom publish in the foundation's *Foreign Policy* magazine of politics and economics. The Endowment provides publications, op-eds, policy papers and books related to its mandate of promoting active international engagement of the U.S. It also provides resources specifically aimed at journalists, policy makers, students and professors.

Center for Defense Information

www.cdi.org

The Washington, D.C.-based Center for Defense Information prides itself on being an independent source of defence-related discussion. The Center is not affiliated with nor does it take donations from military contractors. The Center examines nuclear issues within the context of related concerns, such as the small arms trade, space security and children in armed conflict.

Center for Non-Proliferation Studies

http://cns.miis.edu

Operating in Monterey, California, the Center for Non-Proliferation Studies develops educational content focusing on students and instructors from high school and onwards. The website features online tutorials for use by schools, instructors and institutions. In addition, it has an online database on weapons of mass destruction, terrorism, nuclear trafficking, including country profiles.

Fellowship of Reconciliation

www.forusa.org

Fellowship of Reconciliation is an interfaith initiative to unite the progressive religious communities of Islamic, Jewish, Christian and Buddhist faiths. It provides perspectives on peace and disarmament issues from these principal religions and publishes its bi-monthly publication, *Fellowship*, as a free online magazine. The primary philosophy of the *Fellowship* is that of achieving radical change through non-violent measures, such as education, compassionate action and coalition building.

Global Security Institute

www.gsinstitute.org

The Global Security Institute brings together former heads of state, diplomats, politicians, Nobel laureates, religious leaders and other experts in search of co-operation and security based on the rule of law. The Institute is a co-sponsor of the Middle Powers Initiative and also sponsors the Bipartisan Security Group, which consists of Republican and Democratic nuclear disarmament experts in the United States with backgrounds in law, intelligence and military affairs.

International Peace Bureau

www.ipb.org

The International Peace Bureau describes itself as the "world's oldest and most comprehensive international peace federation" and covers important issues such as human rights and conflict, disarmament, security, peace education, youth and women. The organization was founded in 1892 and in 1910 it was awarded the Nobel Peace Prize. It develops a substantial amount of content devoted to youth and women peacemakers and their accomplishments around the world.

International Physicians for the Prevention of Nuclear War

www.ippnw.org

Winner of the 1985 Nobel Peace Prize, International Physicians for the Prevention of Nuclear War has in the past published *Abolition 2000: Handbook for a World Without Nuclear Weapons*, a handbook for physician activists offering practical suggestions for taking concrete actions. The group also has hypothetical scenarios concerning the health impacts of nuclear explosions in populous areas.

Lawyers' Committee on Nuclear Policy

www.lcnp.org

The Lawyers' Committee for Nuclear Policy is a national non-profit organization based in New York that promotes peace and disarmament through national and international frameworks. It provides legal policy, advice and analysis to activists, policy makers, individuals, organizations and media concerning disarmament and international law.

Los Alamos Study Group

www.lasg.org

The Los Alamos Study Group focuses on the area near the Los Alamos, New Mexico, nuclear waste dump. The group's banner issues include nuclear disarmament, social justice, environmental protection and economic sustainability. It has undertaken various media campaigns involving television, print and radio broadcast advertisements and also produces bumper stickers and yard signs.

Middle Powers Initiative

www.gsinstitute.org/mpi

The Middle Powers Initiative (MPI), sponsored by eight non-governmental bodies, works with middle-power nations to encourage them to use their access to the nuclear weapons states to press them to meet disarmament obligations. The group sponsors the Parliamentary Network for Nuclear Disarmament. MPI's website provides a list of experts on nuclear policy issues as well as links to important documents, reports and publications.

Natural Resources Defense Council

www.nrdc.org

The Natural Resources Defense Council gathers information for researchers interested in clean air, oceans and cities as well as the impact of chemicals and nuclear energy on these areas. The Council issues annual reports as well as periodical analyses and notices for action on these problems.

Non-Governmental Organization (NGO) Committee on Disarmament, Peace and Security

http://disarm.igc.org

The Non-Governmental Organization (NGO) Committee on Disarmament, Peace and Security provides services and facilities to citizen groups concerned with disarmament issues. The organization acts as a liaison between NGOs and the United Nations Secretariat and coordinates the participation of NGOs in formal disarmament meetings at the U.N. The NGO Committee also acts as a clearing house of U.N. disarmament news in its publication, *Disarmament Times*, which provides information for NGOs, researchers, lobbyists and legislators.

Nuclear Age Peace Foundation

www.wagingpeace.org

The Nuclear Age Peace Foundation is a non-partisan, non-profit organization seeking the abolition of nuclear weapons through advocacy, international law and institutions. It organizes annual conferences, campaigns and peace poetry contests aimed at a younger audience.

Nuclear Threat Initiative

www.nti.org

The mission of the Nuclear Threat Initiative is to mitigate the effects of nuclear, biological and chemical weapons around the world and is co-chaired by Ted Turner and Senator Sam Nunn. It provides annual reports and fact sheets on these weapons to give the public access to knowledge about these threats and foster debate beyond the usually rather small circle of experts.

The Parliamentary Network for Nuclear Disarmament

www.gsinstitute.org/pnnd

The Parliamentary Network for Nuclear Disarmament provides a list of worldwide parliamentary bodies and their resolutions, debates, acts and bills pertaining to nuclear disarmament. This information is disseminated through a searchable database and is proving invaluable to researchers seeking primary source materials.

Project Ploughshares Canada

www.ploughshares.ca

Canada's Ecumenical Peace Coalition has operated under the auspices of the Canadian Council of Churches since 1977 to work towards the control, reduction and eventual abolition of nuclear arms. Project Ploughshares issues its quarterly publication, *Ploughshares Monitor*, which contains information on Canadian peace and security matters, nuclear disarmament and alternative security policies. Another publication, *Armed Conflicts Report*, examines the state of war from a global perspective and seeks to go beyond the coverage offered by mainstream media sources.

Reaching Critical Will

www.reachingcriticalwill.org

The name Reaching Critical Will derives from the organization's goal of reaching a critical mass of political will for nuclear disarmament. The organization provides fact sheets, publications and a list of governmental contacts for those willing to work towards nuclear abolition.

Stimson Organization

www.stimson.org

The Stimson Organization is a "nonprofit, nonpartisan institution devoted to enhancing international peace and security" by advocating instruments of peace, security and co-operation as alternatives to instruments of war. Information is disseminated through periodical policy papers, books and special events.

Union of Concerned Scientists

www.ucsusa.org

The Union of Concerned Scientists is comprised of scientists seeking environmentally friendly solutions to problems related to food, automobiles, the environment, energy and security. Specific attention is paid to nuclear "bunker-buster" bombs and the dangers they would pose to human health when and if they were to be used in combat. This is done specifically through the use of an animated simulation based on a Pentagon model of nuclear fallout.

United Nations Disarmament Website

http://disarmament2.un.org

The UN's disarmament website provides information on weapons of mass destruction, landmines, terrorism and conventional arms.

United Nations Institute for Disarmament Research

www.unidir.org

The United Nations Institute for Disarmament Research is an inter-governmental organization within the United Nations that researches disarmament and security issues to help nations think about and develop policies. Its quarterly, bilingual (English and French) journal, *Disarmament Forum,* offers analysis aimed at experts and laypeople with an interest in international security.

Western States Legal Foundation

www.wslfweb.org

Founded in 1982, the Western States Legal Foundation monitors and analyzes U.S. nuclear weapons programs and policies as well as related high technology energy and weapons programs. Its focus is on U.S. national nuclear weapons laboratories. The website features documents that have not been publicized by their originating agencies and governmental bodies. This feature will prove useful for whistle-blowers and watchdogs of nuclear energy, weapons programs as well as overall military activity.

Wisconsin Project on Nuclear Arms Control

www.wisconsinproject.org

The Wisconsin Project on Nuclear Arms Control carries out research and education designed to help stop the spread of nuclear arms. For example, its Risk Report software compiles unclassified information on companies suspected of constructing weapons of mass destruction. The project has also compiled missile profiles of select nations in addition to periodical updates on Iraq and Iran's weapons of mass destruction capabilities.

Appendix

Hiroshima Peace Declaration, 2005

This August 6, the 60th anniversary of the atomic bombing, is a moment of shared lamentation in which more than 300 thousand souls of A-bomb victims and those who remain behind transcend the boundary between life and death to remember that day. It is also a time of inheritance, of awakening, and of commitment, in which we inherit the commitment of the *hibakusha* to the abolition of nuclear weapons and realization of genuine world peace, awaken to our individual responsibilities, and recommit ourselves to take action. This new commitment, building on the desires of all war victims and the millions around the world who are sharing this moment, is creating a harmony that is enveloping our planet.

The keynote of this harmony is the *hibakusha* warning, "No one else should ever suffer as we did," along with the cornerstone of all religions and bodies of law, "Thou shalt not kill." Our sacred obligation to future generations is to establish this axiom, especially its corollary, "Thou shalt not kill children," as the highest priority for the human race across all nations and religions. The International Court of Justice advisory opinion issued nine years ago was a vital step toward fulfilling this obligation, and the Japanese Constitution, which embodies this axiom forever as the sovereign

231

will of a nation, should be a guiding light for the world in the 21st century.

Unfortunately, the Review Conference of the Nuclear Non-Proliferation Treaty this past May left no doubt that the U.S., Russia, U.K., France, China, India, Pakistan, North Korea and a few other nations wishing to become nuclear-weapon states are ignoring the majority voices of the people and governments of the world, thereby jeopardizing human survival.

Based on the dogma "Might is right," these countries have formed their own "nuclear club," the admission requirement being possession of nuclear weapons. Through the media, they have long repeated the incantation, "Nuclear weapons protect you." With no means of rebuttal, many people worldwide have succumbed to the feeling that "There is nothing we can do." Within the United Nations, nuclear club members use their veto power to override the global majority and pursue their selfish objectives.

To break out of this situation, Mayors for Peace, with more than 1,080 member cities, is currently holding its sixth General Conference in Hiroshima, where we are revising the Emergency Campaign to Ban Nuclear Weapons launched two years ago. The primary objective is to produce an action plan that will further expand the circle of cooperation formed by the U.S. Conference of Mayors, the European Parliament, International Physicians for the Prevention of Nuclear War and other international NGOs, organizations and individuals worldwide, and will encourage all world citizens to awaken to their own responsibilities with a sense of urgency, "as if the entire world rests on their shoulders alone," and work with new commitment to abolish nuclear weapons.

To these ends and to ensure that the will of the majority is reflected at the UN, we propose that the First Committee of the UN General Assembly, which will meet in October, establish a special committee to deliberate and plan for the achievement and maintenance of a nuclear-weapon-free world. Such a committee is needed because the Conference on Disarmament in Geneva and the NPT Review Conference in New York have failed due to a "consensus rule" that gives a veto to every country.

We expect that the General Assembly will then act on the recommendations from this special committee, adopting by the year 2010 specific steps leading toward the elimination of nuclear weapons by 2020.

Meanwhile, we hereby declare the 369 days from today until August 9, 2006, a "Year of Inheritance, Awakening and Commitment." During this Year, the Mayors for Peace, working with nations, NGOs and the vast majority of the world's people, will launch a great diversity of campaigns for nuclear weapons abolition in numerous cities throughout the world.

We expect the Japanese government to respect the voice of the world's cities and work energetically in the First Committee and the General Assembly to ensure that the abolition of nuclear weapons is achieved by the will of the majority. Furthermore, we request that the Japanese government provide the warm, humanitarian support appropriate to the needs of all the aging *hibakusha*, including those living abroad and those exposed in areas affected by the black rain.

On this, the sixtieth anniversary of the atomic bombing, we seek to comfort the souls of all its victims by declaring that we humbly reaffirm our responsibility never to "repeat the evil."

"Please rest peacefully; for we will not repeat the evil."

August 6, 2005

Tadatoshi Akiba
Mayor
The City of Hiroshima

Index of Proper Names and Organizations

A

J

M

N

W

X

Y

Z

THE HUMAN RIGHT *to Peace*

DOUGLAS ROCHE

ISBN 2-89507-409-7

The peoples of the Earth have a sacred right to peace. This is the conviction and the theme of *The Human Right to Peace*, by Douglas Roche, who builds upon a long career in politics, diplomacy and social activism in examining the requirements for peace in the post–September 11 world. The Right to Peace has already been defined by the United Nations, but its meaning has been muted by the continuation of the war culture. The U.N. is now working to animate the Right to Peace so it can finally take its place among the other recognized human rights that breath life into the international system.

Some discount the emerging right to peace and doubt that it can be achieved in a world driven by an excessive militarism that was re-vivified in the aftermath of the 9/11 terrorist attacks. Roche turns the prevailing logic on its head by showing that wars are not inevitable and that the modern world possesses the creativity and political and legal instruments to resolve conflict without war. Achieving this goal is within our reach, but it requires a fundamental change in our attitudes.